Entrepreneur

FUND YOUR BUSINESS

SMART STRATEGIES TO SECURE FINANCING

BY THE STAFF OF ENTREPRENEUR MEDIA

Entrepreneur Press®

Entrepreneur Press, Publisher
Cover Design: Andrew Welyczko
Production and Composition: Faith & Family Publications

This publication is designed to provide accurate and authoritative information
in regard to the subject matter covered. It is sold with the understanding that the
publisher is not engaged in rendering legal, accounting, or other professional
services. If legal advice or other expert assistance is required, the services of a
competent professional person should be sought.

Entrepreneur Press® is a registered trademark of Entrepreneur Media, LLC

Library of Congress Cataloging-in-Publication Data
   Names: Entrepreneur Media, LLC, issuing body.
   Title: Fund your business : smart strategies to secure financing / The
      Staff of Entrepreneur Media.
   Description: Irvine : Entrepreneur Press, [2024] | Includes index. |
      Summary: "This book gives you the inside scoop on how to get the money
      you need to start, run, and grow your business"-- Provided by publisher.
   Identifiers: LCCN 2023042574 (print) | LCCN 2023042575 (ebook) | ISBN
      9781642011609 (paperback) | ISBN 9781613084717 (epub)
   Subjects: LCSH: New business enterprises. | Small business--Finance. |
      Small business--Management.
   Classification: LCC HD62.5 .F86 2024 (print) | LCC HD62.5 (ebook) | DDC
      658.1/1--dc23/eng/20240104
   LC record available at https://lccn.loc.gov/2023042574
   LC ebook record available at https://lccn.loc.gov/2023042575

Printed in the United States of America

27 26 25 24   10 9 8 7 6 5 4 3 2 1

Contents

CHAPTER 7

Crowdfunding Like a Champ 127

CHAPTER 8

Scouting the Alternative Lending Landscape 151

CHAPTER 9

Wooing Angels and Venture Capitalists................... 165

Preface

Starting a business is a journey. From the moment you come up with an idea for the next great product or service to the ribbon cutting and grand opening, you will travel a long, sometimes winding, road toward success. And like any other trip you take in life, this one costs money. While many startups begin with cash already in the bank (lucky them!), most aspiring entrepreneurs have to somehow come up with the cash to build their dreams, whether they choose to borrow, bootstrap, crowdfund, or go with venture capital.

That's where we come in. The writers and editors at Entrepreneur research the latest trends in small business and startup funding and speak with the people who pursue their startup dreams, as well as those who help those dreams become reality. In this book, we've compiled a lot of this advice, along with stories from the trenches from those who have gone before you in the search for business funding. You will read about entrepreneurs who leveraged their life savings and made investors of family members, and those who got their funding through successful venture capital presentations or pitch slams. Some of these startup stories have happy endings involving IPOs or corporate buyouts, while others end with the realization that dreams don't always come true. But all of these stories share a common thread: No one makes it without a little help, whether that help comes from friends or loan officers.

This book gives you the inside scoop on how to get the money you need. You'll discover dozens of sources of capital. You'll learn secrets to funding your business yourself, tapping into the most common source of startup financing (family and friends), discovering sources you may never have thought of to look for money, and turning to the crowd for funding.

You will learn about several different options, starting with the pros and pitfalls of bootstrapping while growing your business using tactics like bartering and exploring free services. Do you stand a chance of getting venture capital or attracting private investors? You'll find out after reading stories from investors who know the ropes. And if you're looking for a loan, look no further for the keys to finding the right bank or other lending institution. This book explains what bankers look for when evaluating a loan application—and offers valuable tips for making sure yours meets the mark. What about money from Uncle Sam? Yes, it exists. You'll learn about loan programs from the government, including special assistance for women and minority entrepreneurs. Whatever your particular situation, you're sure to find great tips and tricks here.

Are you ready? Your journey begins now.

CHAPTER 1

Introduction

You're excited to start a business. Maybe you have a specific idea, or maybe you're just fascinated with the idea of launching and growing your own enterprise. You're willing to take some risks, like leaving your current job or going without a paycheck for a while. But there's one tiny logistical hurdle stopping you: You don't have much money.

On the surface, this seems like a major problem—but a lack of personal capital shouldn't stop you from pursuing your dreams. In fact, it's entirely possible to start and grow a business with almost *no* personal financial investment whatsoever, if you know what you're doing.

Why does a business need money in the first place? That depends on the business. It's not like there's a uniform "startup fee" for building a business. Different businesses will have different needs. So, the first step is to consider the kind of business you are proposing and then think thoroughly about what it would take to get it up and running. It's important to start putting your dream in writing. Then you should be able to come up with at least a ballpark estimate of how much money you will need. And then you can start looking into particular methods to fund your company.

Outlining a Basic Business Plan

There are lots of books about creating business plans, and that's not the focus of this book, so we won't spend a lot of time on this. Don't worry too much about making it perfect right off the bat. It doesn't have to be rocket science. But you need to start somewhere.

Here is a suggested outline for a basic business plan:

1. **Executive summary:** An overview of the plan that should include a brief description of the company, its products or services, the target market, and financial projections. You may want to write this part last, once you rough out the other parts. Spend some time polishing your words here, as it's the first thing anybody will read.
2. **Company description:** Write more details about your company, including its ownership structure, mission statement, goals, proposed size, and employment plans.
3. **Market analysis:** Describe the market you plan to enter, including information on its size and growth, key players, and trends. You can fire up your favorite search engine for this, or investigate locally— or both. And be honest in your assessment. You may discover the market that you thought needed you is already saturated and you need to tweak your plans. That's valuable info for you. Analyze your competitors, especially looking for their weak points, and describe how your company will be differentiated from them.
4. **Customer analysis:** Who will be buying your products or services? Identify and describe who they are and what their needs are. Then explain how your products or services will meet those needs better than the competition.

5. **Your products or services:** Describe the products or services you will offer, including features and benefits, pricing, and how you will make or deliver them.

6. **Marketing and sales:** How will you get the word out about your new business? Outline your ideas for promoting and selling your products or services to your target market. Talk about and estimate your sales and marketing budget. Research what you think might be the best ways of reaching out, whether that's radio spots, flyers left on doors, or online promotions on social media (or all of them).

7. **Day-to-day operations:** Describe how your company will be run on a day-to-day basis, including the processes for producing your products or services and any plans for expanding in the future.

8. **Financial Projections:** Provide projected financial statements for the next three to five years, including a profit and loss statement, balance sheet, and cash flow statement.

9. **Appendices:** Include any additional information that supports your business plan, such as resumes of key employees, product samples, or market research data.

Remember, your business plan is a living document that will evolve as your business grows and changes, so be prepared to revise and update it regularly.

For assistance in creating a winning business plan, grab a copy of *Write Your Business Plan, Second Edition* (Entrepreneur Press). This step-by-step guide will help you build and launch the business of your dreams (entrepreneur.com/bookstore/isbn/9781642011586/write-your-business-plan).

Consider the costs involved:

▷ *Licenses and permits.* Depending on where you live, you may need special paperwork and registrations to operate.
▷ *Supplies.* Are you buying raw materials? What about office supplies?

> *Equipment.* Do you need specialized machinery or software? Do you need computers and/or other electronic devices?
> *Office space.* This is a huge potential expense, and don't forget about things like internet and utility costs.
> *Associations, subscriptions, memberships.* What publications will you subscribe to, and what professional organizations will you need to join?
> *Operating expenses.* Dig into the nooks and crannies here, and don't forget about marketing.
> *Legal fees.* Are you consulting a lawyer throughout your business development process?
> *Employees and contractors.* If you can't do it alone, you'll need people on your payroll.

Before you approach the bank, make sure you have a good handle on how much cash you actually need. Once you know what and how much you need, then you can start considering how to get it.

The best way to determine this is to create a monthly cash flow projection. We've included a cash flow projection worksheet (Figure 1.1 on page 5) for your convenience.

Cash-Flow Worksheet

	Month 1	Month 2	Month 3	Month 4	Month 5	Month 6	Month 7	Month 8	Month 9	Month 10	Month 11	Month 12	Total Year 1
Cash Available:													
Net Income after Taxes													
Depreciation													
Amortization													
Decrease in A/R													
Decrease in Inventory													
Increase in Accounts Payable													
Increase in Notes Payable-ST													
Increase in Long-Term Debt													
Decrease in Other Assets													
Increase in Other Liabilities													
Total Cash Available													
Cash Disbursements													
Owners' Draw/Dividends													
Increase in A/R													
Increase in Inventory													
Decrease in Accounts Payable													
Capital Expenditures													
Decrease in Notes Payable-ST													
Current Maturities of Long-Term Debt													
Increase in Other Assets													
Decrease in Other Liabilities													
Total Cash Disbursements													
Monthly Cash Flow													
Cumulative Cash Flow													

Figure 1.1. Cash Flow Worksheet

The cash flow worksheet will give you a realistic picture of your funding needs. For example, if your customer pays you in 60 days, but you have to pay your vendors in 15 days, you might need some extra money to tide you over. "It will reflect poorly on you if you come into the bank asking for $50,000, then they ask you to create a cash flow projection and you find out that you actually need $100,000," says Adam Hoeksema, cofounder of Indiana-based ProjectionHub, a web app to help entrepreneurs make financial projections. "You should know how much you need and how you will use the funds before approaching the bank." The worksheet in Figure 1.2 on pages 7–8 can help you determine how much cash your startup business may need.

Startup Costs Worksheet

The following two worksheets will help you to compute your initial cash requirements for your business. They list the things you need to consider when determining your startup costs and include both the one-time initial expenses to open your doors and the ongoing costs you'll face during the first 90 days.

Startup Capital Requirements

One-Time Startup Expenses

Startup Expenses	Description	Amount
Advertising	Promotion for opening the business	
Starting inventory	Amount of inventory required to open	
Building construction	Amount per contractor bid and other costs	
Cash	Amount needed for the cash register	
Decorating	Estimate based on bid, if appropriate	
Deposits	Check with utility companies	
Fixtures and equipment	Use actual bids	
Insurance	Bid from insurance agent	
Lease payments	Fees to be paid before opening	
Licenses and permits	Check with city or state offices	
Miscellaneous	All other costs	
Professional fees	Include CPA, attorney, etc.	
Remodeling	Use contractor bids	
Rent	Fee to be paid before opening	
Services	Cleaning, accounting, etc.	
Signs	Use contractor bids	
Supplies	Office, cleaning, etc.	
Unanticipated expenses	Include an amount for the unexpected	
Other		
Other		
Total Startup Costs		$

Figure 1.2. Startup Costs Worksheet

Startup Costs Worksheet

Startup Capital Requirements

Ongoing Monthly Expenses*

Startup Expenses	Description	Amount
Advertising		
Bank service fees		
Credit card charges		
Delivery fees		
Dues and subscriptions		
Insurance	Exclude amount on preceding page	
Interest		
Inventory	See ** below	
Lease payments	Exclude amount on preceding page	
Loan payments	Principal and interest payments	
Office expenses		
Payroll other than owner		
Payroll taxes		
Professional fees		
Rent	Exclude amount on preceding page	
Repairs and maintenance		
Sales tax		
Supplies		
Telephone		
Utilities		
Your salary	Only if applicable during the first three months	
Other		
Total Ongoing Costs		$
Total Startup Costs	Amount from preceding page	$
Total Cash Needed		$

*Include the first three months' cash needs unless otherwise noted.

**Include amount required for inventory expansion. If inventory is to be replaced from cash sales, do not include here. Assume sales will generate enough cash for replacements.

Figure 1.2. Startup Costs Worksheet, continued

The Basics of Obtaining Funding

To start a business with very little money, you can either lower your costs, increase your available capital, or do both.

Your first option is to change your business model to make fewer demands, as listed above. For example, you could reduce your "employee" expenses by being the sole employee at the start. You could work from home instead of renting office space. You can even do your homework to find cheaper sources of supplies, or cut out entire planned product lines that are too expensive to produce at the outset. There are a few expenses that you won't be able to avoid, however; licensing and legal fees will set you back even if you cut back on everything else. But according to the Small Business Administration (SBA), many microbusinesses get started on less than $3,000, and home-based franchises can be started for as little as $1,000.

Your second option invokes the idea of a "warm-up" period for your business. Instead of going straight into full-fledged business mode, you might launch a blog and one niche service, reducing your scope, your audience, and your profit in order to get a head start while slowly ramping up your business. If you start as a self-employed individual, you'll avoid some of the biggest initial costs (and enjoy a simpler tax situation, too). Once you start realizing some revenue, you can reinvest it and build the business you imagined piece by piece, rather than all at once.

Your third option, and the main topic of this book, is securing funding from outside sources. There is nothing wrong with venture capitalist funding. There is a time, stage, and type of startup that's suitable for this approach. But for the majority of entrepreneurs, venture capital is not the best path to obtaining funds. Now is a unique time of financial innovation, when customers can fund entrepreneurs' plans. There are low-interest lending platforms. And for the first time in decades, business owners can advertise that they are raising capital (thanks to Title II of the JOBS Act).

With technological advances, the social media explosion, and the numerous crowdfunding solutions available, it may be that only a small amount of capital is needed to build a minimum viable product. Then the entrepreneur can get out there in the market to test ideas and grow a business. Finding funding is now squarely in entrepreneurial hands.

There are dozens of ways to raise this money, called *capital*, even if you don't have much yourself. Here are just a few potential sources:

- ❯ *Bootstrapping.* Before you seek capital from others, you need to truly explore everything you can do on your own. This can actually help you get financing from other sources later on.
- ❯ *Bank loans.* You can open a line of credit with the bank if your credit is in good standing.
- ❯ *Friends and family.* Don't rule out getting help from friends and family, even if you have to piece the capital together from multiple sources. This can be tricky, though, since if the business fails you risk straining the personal relationship.
- ❯ *Contests and grants.* Yes, there is such a thing as free money, and there are ways to improve your odds of getting it. There are dozens of contests every year in the United States that award startup money to promising new businesses. And the SBA and a number of state and local government agencies exist solely to help small businesses grow. Many of these offer loans and grants to help you get started.
- ❯ *Incubators and accelerators.* These are competitive programs that offer much more than money—although they offer that, too. They provide expertise, networking, and other invaluable help to fledgling businesses.
- ❯ *Crowdfunding.* It's popular for a reason: With a good idea and some hard work, you can attract funding for just about anything.
- ❯ *Alternative lenders.* Many companies and entrepreneurs are trying to provide small businesses with the capital they need through some truly creative and even revolutionary methods. You just need to know where to look.
- ❯ *Angel investors and venture capitalists.* Angel investors are wealthy individuals and firms that back business ideas early on. They typically invest in exchange for partial ownership of the company, which may or may not be a sacrifice worth considering. Venture capitalists are similar, but are typically partnerships or organizations and tend to scout existing businesses looking to expand.
- ❯ *VC alternatives and other investors.* We live in a unique time of financial innovation, when even customers can fund entrepreneurs' plans; there

are low-interest lending platforms; and, for the first time in decades, business owners can advertise that they are raising capital.

By exploring the options discussed in this book, you may be able to reduce your personal financial investment to almost nothing. You may have to make some other sacrifices, such as starting small, accommodating partners, or taking on debt, but if you believe in your business idea, none of these obstacles should stand in your way. Capital is a major hurdle to overcome, but make no mistake—it can be overcome.

The kind of company you want to build will dictate where you turn for capital and when. Running a one-person operation is very different from creating a 100-employee company from the ground up. Likewise, a triple-bottom-line B Corporation that places as much emphasis on community, employees, and environment as it does on profits is a very different beast from a startup with the primary goal of cashing out after several years.

You also need to think about what your unique needs are and where all this is headed. Are you building a lifestyle or a freelance business? A service agency? Something much bigger that you hope will take the world by storm? Do you plan to include some sort of social impact right into your for-profit business model—say, by giving away one product for every one you sell or only hiring veterans? Or is giving back to the community and society at large something you'd prefer to address later, once you've started making revenue? What do you see as your exit strategy? Having your children take over your business several decades from now? Your employees gaining control through an employee ownership program? A nice, big acquisition check? Something else? Your answers to these questions may dictate whose money you pursue to fund your business, and when.

It may seem impossible, but one way or another, you need to believe you will find the funding your business needs to get off the ground and succeed. You have a lot of options—probably far more than you thought. The rest of this book is dedicated to exploring those options to see which ones are best suited to you and your vision.

CHAPTER 2

Going It Alone: Bootstrapping Like a Boss

The old saying "pull yourself up by your bootstraps" describes, of course, something that's literally impossible. You can try it—put on some boots, grab your bootstraps, and pull up as hard as you can. If you're like most people, this procedure will fail to suspend the law of gravity, and you will remain firmly planted on the earth. But in the financial world, bootstrapping isn't just possible; it's recommended. It means funding yourself as much as possible. The reasons you should try to fund your own business before seeking outside capital ought to be obvious. Lenders and investors want to see your business thesis proven before they pony up any cash.

Investors also like to see that founders have some skin in the game—they like entrepreneurs who've put it all on the line.

There's also something to be said for bootstrapping as long as you can so that you're forced to bring in revenue as quickly as possible. Outside investments tend to make business owners comfortable with overspending—money that comes from someone else is somehow easier to spend. Without the hunger bootstrapping brings, it's tempting to put off making revenue for another month, quarter, or even year.

10 Bootstrapping Tips to Turn Your Idea into Reality

Although venture capitalists (VCs) are often assumed to be the primary source of funding for startups, this is a myth. In reality, the vast majority of startups are funded without capital injections from venture capitalists or angel investors. The real numbers are eye-opening—VCs fund only 0.05 percent of startups, and angel investors are responsible for funding just 0.91 percent. Take a moment to really think about those percentages in relation to the half million or so new businesses started each month in the United States.

With the chances of receiving funding so slim, if you are serious about turning your idea into a reality, you are most likely going to have to dip into your own pockets and bootstrap your way to the top. It isn't easy, but it can be very rewarding, both personally and financially, as you retain 100 percent of your equity.

In no particular order, here are 10 tips to help you bootstrap your way to success.

1. *Fully Research Your Market and Competition*

Before you do anything else, you need to make sure you have a viable business opportunity. Is your proposed product or service already available on the market? If there is competition, how will consumers differentiate between you and them? What makes you better? What is your unique selling point?

Some highly successful software-as-a-service companies have sold their product before they even developed it, to be completely certain there was a market for it. This isn't the conventional way to do it, but it's an example of entrepreneurs going to extremes to be 100 percent positive they had a winner before going all in.

2. Create a Business Model That Produces Quick Revenue

If you are bootstrapping, you need to make sure your business model generates revenue quickly. If not, you will be dead in the water once you blow through your reserves. Constant cash flow is mandatory—if you look at successful bootstrapped startups, you will see they all generated revenue very quickly.

3. Handle Your Own Public Relations in the Beginning

Startups can benefit greatly from major media exposure in the beginning, but journalists and editors receive press kits from PR firms around the clock. They don't want to talk to a public relations representative—they want to talk to you! They are much more interested in speaking with a founder than a PR firm, because they want to hear your story just as much as they want to hear about your actual startup.

There are a number of ways for startups to score media coverage, so roll up your sleeves and get cracking.

4. Provide Ways for Your Initial Customers and Early Adopters to Create Buzz

People love new startups and technologies, and they love to show the world that they are cool, hip, and trendy through social media. Provide ways for your early customers to help put your startup in front of their social audiences.

Allow them to unlock a discount coupon by sharing your website on social media or create a branded hashtag and randomly select winners for prizes. You can even share images of your customers using your product with a designated hashtag on the company social media pages. By appealing to people's egos, you can create instant brand engagement.

5. Don't Be Afraid to Let Your Website Grow with You

It happens all the time—a startup has a custom website designed, and by the time all the features are built out, they have no marketing dollars left.

They use their entire pile of seed money on a great website but then have no way of marketing it—and they turn into a statistic, joining the 80 percent of businesses that fail within their first 18 months.

If you are operating on a shoestring budget, you can use a premade theme to get you off the ground and use the majority of your funds to promote and grow your business. Once you have positive cash flow and a proven business model, revamp your website.

6. *Launch Creative Branding and Marketing Campaigns*

You don't always have to have the deepest pockets to get brand exposure—you just need a creative approach. A great example is Newcastle Brown Ale's video about almost making a Super Bowl commercial with Anna Kendrick. The company didn't purchase expensive airtime for the Super Bowl, but it did release a video about how it almost did. The video went viral on social media and got more publicity than an actual commercial would have.

7. *Account for Every Penny You Spend*

Keeping track of every penny that leaves your business is crucial. Money vanishes quickly when you start a business. Sloppy accounting can lead to a rude awakening. Use accounting software, such as QuickBooks, or free tools, such as Mint, that will help keep track of your spending and gauge burn rate. Monitor your cash daily—there is no excuse for lazy accounting.

8. *Eliminate as Many Personal Expenses as Possible*

When bootstrapping a startup, there isn't a nice comfortable salary that comes with the gig—you have to be prepared to drastically prune unnecessary expenses or eliminate them altogether.

Substitute public transportation for a huge car payment, take on a roommate or two to reduce living expenses, brew your own morning cup of coffee instead of opting for a $4 cup at the local coffeehouse, cancel your cable and streaming subscriptions. Look at your personal bank statements for the past few months to uncover areas where you might reduce or eliminate expenses.

9. *Do as Many Jobs by Yourself as You Can in the Beginning*

There is a big difference between jobs you can't do and jobs you simply don't want to do. If a task requires specific technical knowledge you don't possess, then of course delegate it—but if it's something you are fully capable of but just don't feel like doing, you are creating an unnecessary expense. Do whatever you have to do to make your business succeed, whether that's making sales calls or emptying the trash.

10. *Be Persistent and Don't Give Up*

When you are just starting out, there will be many obstacles to overcome. Suppliers and vendors aren't always overly excited to work with brand-new companies, and building consumer trust can be a challenge. You have to be persistent. Kick down doors and dial the phone nonstop to make connections and build relationships. Don't take rejection personally—it is going to happen.

Bootstrapping a business isn't an easy task. It's very challenging—but not impossible.

Balancing Act: Starting Up without Quitting Your Day Job

Erica Zidel knew that trying to raise funds for her startup would be a full-time job. She worried that chasing after capital would distract her from building the best product she could. So, rather than sweat the investment game, she spent years holding down a day job while bootstrapping her new company on the side.

"I've basically been working two full-time jobs," says Zidel, founder and CEO of Sitting Around, an online community that makes it easy for parents to find and coordinate babysitting co-ops in their neighborhoods. It's a hectic schedule—schizophrenic, even—but it's also thrilling. "When I woke up this morning, I realized that it was Monday, and I got excited," Zidel says.

What's perhaps more thrilling is that she's been able to self-fund Sitting Around with the money she earns from her consulting work. Besides avoiding getting sidetracked with fundraising, Zidel and her business partner, CTO Ted Tieken, have been able to retain 100 percent ownership of the babysitting venture.

"Bootstrapping early on means I have complete control over the vision and the product at a time when even small changes can lead to big consequences down the road," Zidel says. "I wanted the flexibility to make the right decisions, free from a board or an investor's influence. When you have just the founders making decisions, you can innovate much faster."

That focus on innovation has paid off. Sitting Around serves families in the United States as well as several countries abroad. Since the site launched in 2010, its user base has taken off. In 2011, Sitting Around was also one of 125 finalists in MassChallenge, a Boston-based startup competition and accelerator program. Perhaps most exciting of all, shortly after launching the company, Zidel was honored at the White House as a champion of change for her contributions to child care.

The beauty of moonlighting with a startup is that it lets you test a business idea without jeopardizing your financial well-being, says Pamela Slim, business consultant and author of *Escape from Cubicle Nation: From Corporate Prisoner to Thriving Entrepreneur.*

"When you don't know where your monthly income is coming from, it often sets up a fight-or-flight response in your brain," Slim says. "And that's not a good place to be when you're trying to be creative. So having that psychological cushion is often very important for the development of business ideas."

Zidel will attest to that. Thanks to her day job, she's been able to pour $15,000 to $20,000 of her own money into her business. Not having to take on debt or live like a monk has been a point of pride—but it has also been a necessity. "Since I'm a mother, I have to maintain an adequate standard of living for my son," Zidel explains. "While I'm definitely frugal and very conscious that a dollar spent on lifestyle is a dollar not spent on Sitting Around, I'd rather work two jobs than feed my son ramen."

Indeed, balancing a day job with the time and effort that goes into launching a startup business is not for the faint of heart. But don't let that discourage you—it can be done. Here are some tips for facing this challenge without burning out, abandoning other areas of your life, or throwing in the towel.

Juggling Act

Bootstrapping a business is not without its challenges. Besides the long hours and the strain on personal relationships, it can be tricky to split one's creative juices between two professional pursuits.

"Being pulled in multiple directions is the hardest," says Zidel. "It takes a while for your brain to switch gears. And when things start to collide, it can be hard to say [what] you should be working on."

To stay productive and sane, Zidel schedules her workdays down to the hour and sticks to a list of nonnegotiable items to accomplish each day. Still, she admits, "It's hard to stop working. I really have to force myself to carve out some personal time."

Bootstrapping with income earned not from a single employer, but from a cadre of consulting clients comes with its own set of obstacles.

"Sometimes customers require a lot of attention, making it difficult to carve out time for your startup," says Aaron Franklin, cofounder of LazyMeter.com, a web-based productivity tool that ultimately went out of business in 2013. Likewise, he adds, "When you start consulting, it can be tempting to work as many hours as they can pay you."

Either way, your startup loses—which is why it's important to make an exit plan and stick to it. After LazyMeter failed to move forward, Franklin went on to work for Pinterest and Turi as a product manager and now works for Apple as a product manager. "If you make enough revenue to last another month but slow down your startup by a month, you're not getting ahead," Franklin says. "Make sure your efforts are moving you forward, not backward."

Knowing When to Leap

How will you know when to quit your day job? Author Pamela Slim advises that once you've tested your idea in the real world and know there's a market for it, you should set specific, tangible metrics.

"For some people, it can be getting a significant amount of traffic on their website or selling a certain number of units," she says. "For some people, it's when they have X dollars in their savings. For some people, it's a date—say, 'Come hell or high water, December 31, I'm quitting my job.'"

For Nick Cronin, former cofounder and CEO of ExpertBids.com, which connected business owners with lawyers, CPAs, and other consultants, the day came when his web startup began to bring in revenue. After spending 15 months growing his site to 10,000 users—7,000 of them experts—Cronin left his gig as a corporate attorney to work on his startup full time. Shortly after, he said, "We [were bringing] in enough money for a developer and myself to work on [the site] and to cover all expenses, including office space and advertising/marketing."

Before quitting his job, Cronin spent a year lining his savings account. "I knew that things were going to take time and that we were going to need a little bit of a runway before I could take a salary," says the Chicago-based entrepreneur. "My goal was to have nine months where, if we didn't make a dollar, I'd be totally fine."

The escape route looks completely different for Zidel. "It's less the number of users and more the rate of growth. We've been testing different components of our business to see what works before we go out to raise money and turn the gas on," she says. "Now we have a lot of great data: what messages resonate, what products make money."

To those who say you're not a true entrepreneur unless you quit your day job, Zidel cries foul. "A lot of people think that to be a successful entrepreneur, you need to be sleeping on an air mattress and working on your business 80 to 90 hours a week," she says. "But I think that definition of success is silly. I'm living proof that if you have a quality idea and you spend your time well and execute it well, you can wind up with something great."

Protecting Your Rep at Your Day Job

Your boss may not be thrilled to learn that you're cultivating a side business. To avoid biting the hand that feeds you, follow this advice from Pamela Slim:

> ❯ *Check your employment agreement and employee handbook.* Some companies have a no-moonlighting policy. Others have noncompete agreements that prohibit you from doing your own business with their clients. Others—particularly technology companies—even have policies that nab the intellectual property rights of anything you create even on your own time.

⟩ *Keep quiet about your side project.* Unless your employment agreement requires you to come clean about your after-hours venture, Slim recommends staying mum with managers and colleagues. Yes, some might be supportive of your side pursuit. But, Slim says, once the cat's out of the bag, "Be prepared to be fired as a worst-case scenario."

⟩ *Don't work on your startup on company time.* Just because you love your side project more than your job, that doesn't give you license to slack off at work. Resist the urge to use your work phone and email to conduct startup business. "Take the calls on your cell on a break, and, if possible, use your own laptop or mobile device to check personal email," Slim says. "Remember, everything is tracked and monitored in large corporations."

⟩ *Don't burn bridges.* Guard your professional reputation as though your life depends on it. "It's never a pleasant thing to be fired for performance," Slim says. "That's not the way you want to go out." Besides, your current employer might be a future customer or investor.

When to Scrimp and When to Splurge

James DiSabatino was the quintessential bootstrapper. He used all his savings—plus a $20,000 loan from his dad—to start Roxy's Grilled Cheese, the first food truck to park on city property in Boston. Aside from the fee to form a limited liability company (LLC), his main startup cost was the 12-year-old hot dog truck he bought for $45,000.

"I spent every last dime just on the truck itself," DiSabatino says of the mobile kitchen he initially used to cook and sell the gourmet sandwiches and sides that put his business on the map. He had no publicist, slick website, or grand-opening event. Just the artisanal ingredients he purchased daily to make enough "next level" grilled cheese sandwiches to stay in business another day.

For the first three months, DiSabatino worked 20 hours a day, five days a week, tending bar on his two days off for fast cash. At the time, he had one employee, a pal he paid $10 an hour to help run the truck, plus half a dozen friends and family members who pitched in during lunch crunches, often without pay.

To trim personal expenses, DiSabatino lived in his car for a month, then with his parents for another eight. "I slept in the back seat," he says. "I still keep a pillow there to remind myself what I used to do for my company."

That frugality paid off. Within three years, Roxy's Grilled Cheese had two food trucks, 30 employees, a catering arm, and a sit-down fast-casual restaurant serving its signature sandwiches, beer, and wine. The company was also featured on Food Network's *The Great Food Truck Race* in 2011. DiSabatino has added a vegetarian fast-casual restaurant to his resume as well, opening Whole Heart Provisions in 2015 and in December 2016 he partnered with Area Four to open Boston's first arcade bar, A4cade.

Of course, you don't have to live in a van down by the river to achieve startup liftoff, but you do have to carefully ration every dollar you spend (or charge). That said, some early-stage outlay to protect, promote, and grow a sustainable company is well worth the splurge. Consider these your bootstrapping nonnegotiables. Without them, you may not have a business to run for very long.

Respect Law and (Financial) Order

Springing for the necessary legal and financial services to sufficiently protect your company is a must, whether you need help with contracts, patents, trademarks, articles of incorporation, taxes, bookkeeping, or financial reports. How much you pay for those services—and to whom—is up for debate.

DiSabatino went straight to the source to form an LLC, paying the state of Massachusetts $500 online. At the time, he didn't see the need to retain an attorney. He says it wasn't until Roxy's "started to grow and needed to have the infrastructure" that he hired one.

Melani Gordon, CEO of TapHunter, which provides web and mobile tools for the bar and beverage industry, has a different take. "Cheapness isn't always the best," the San Diego serial entrepreneur says. When a mentor connected Gordon and her cofounder with a law firm willing to work pro bono, "we thought we were getting the deal of the century," she says. Instead, the entrepreneurs found themselves shuffled between legal interns, whose work was riddled with mistakes.

Frustrated, Gordon hired a more responsive law firm experienced with tech startups. Sure, it was hard to shell out hundreds of bucks per hour, but "setting up your legal entity and your business properly is one of the most important steps," she says.

Gordon had to learn the same lesson when it came to managing her books. Initially, she tried using the bookkeeper from her previous company, a small marketing agency she ran for nearly a decade. But that didn't go smoothly, so she upgraded to a CPA who had worked with tech startups.

"You need to find a service provider who has worked with your type of business before," Gordon says. A bookkeeper who has experience only with construction companies, for example, may not be the best fit for a retail shop or a tech venture.

People Pay for Quality and So Should You

There's a fine line between saving on materials and selling customers short. Getting the best possible deal on the highest caliber of materials to deliver a winning product is key, says Scott Gerber, founder of Young Entrepreneur Council (YEC), an invitation-only organization that comprises more than 1,500 U.S. entrepreneurs ages 40 and younger. "If the initial product ends up being terrible—even if your future product is going to be better—it's going to put a bad taste in people's mouths," says Gerber, author of *Never Get a "Real" Job: How to Dump Your Boss, Build a Business, and Not Go Broke.*

Compromising on quality was never an option for DiSabatino. From day one, he went out of his way to serve high-quality cheeses, meats, breads, and condiments sourced fresh from local vendors. "We wanted to surprise people with how good our food was," he says. "We weren't going to be able to do that by skimping on ingredients."

Restaurants aren't the only startups with high standards, though. Consider Buzzy, a pain-blocking device for children afraid of shots developed by Amy Baxter, a pediatric emergency doctor and CEO and founder of MMJ Labs. "All we scrimp on is cheaper paper for our instructions," says Baxter. For example, she says, Buzzy's internal mechanics are "obnoxiously expensive," twice as much as any other she tested when prototyping the product. "But none of the other motors I've tried actually relieve pain."

On the flip side, expensive does not always mean better. Baxter laments a decision to replace the low-cost tourniquets she used to include with her product with $40,000 worth of high-end silicone straps. It turned out that medical professionals preferred the disposable tourniquets they already had at their own facilities (which are five times cheaper), and customers using Buzzy at home preferred the Velcro straps shipped with earlier versions of the product (1.75 times cheaper). "I should have market-tested first," she says. Ultimately, Baxter found what worked, and Buzzy has gone mainstream, now used by more than a quarter million patients, in more than 5,000 hospitals and clinics, with more than 75,000 units sold.

Know Where Your Customers Are

How you spend your early marketing dollars to generate leads will vary depending on what you're selling and to whom. Gerber recommends that when selling directly to consumers, focus on marketing tactics that attract the largest swath. "You need to get to the lowest-hanging fruit as quickly as possible," he says.

This might mean taking preorders via a crowdfunding platform or from your own website. It might mean buying web banner ads or signing up for Google AdWords. It might mean exhibiting your product or service at a local trade show. For Sean Moore, founder of SMART College Funding, a financial planning company in Boca Raton, Florida, that helps high-net-worth families reduce college costs, it meant spending $5,000 on printed brochures that potential clients could take home.

Having "something physical" to hand out at school and parent group presentations is important to Moore, a certified financial planner who started SMART College in 2011. "If I tell them to look on my website, I'm putting the onus on them," Moore says. "It's not their responsibility to find out who I am." Instead, he prefers to hand out information that people can ponder at their leisure and easily share with family members.

If you're selling to businesses rather than to individuals, your top marketing priority should be meeting with potential customers face-to-face, Gerber says. "You're not trying to build a massive funnel; you're trying to get into a room and shake someone's hand," he explains. Any early-stage marketing costs that don't produce this outcome aren't worth it.

For Baxter, spending thousands of dollars on a ticket to TEDMED, an annual conference for health and medicine innovations, yields some of the highest ROI. There, she gets to connect with dozens of heavy hitters in the health-care industry, such as international laboratory network Quest Diagnostics, which stocks all 2,000-plus of its U.S. clinics with Baxter's pain management products.

Build a Solid Tech Foundation

It's tough to run a startup today without a web and mobile presence. Fortunately, the internet is brimming with accessible, affordable digital tools that can get you up and running in a matter of hours.

"Figure out what's available to get you into the game at an inexpensive level," Gerber says. "If there's something that can build you a website for $9.95 a month so you can get started, use it. You don't need designers or web engineers until you have a viable proof of concept."

Money Pits: Rein in Expenses in These Areas

Here are some ideas for areas where you can potentially save money:

- **Office space.** Unless you're running a storefront, you have no business leasing an office, says Gerber. Stick to basements, garages, kitchen tables, and cafés early on. If you need to meet a client, rent an hourly meeting space or conference room.

- **Marketing.** If you don't need a $5,000 logo or a $10,000 website to attract and retain your first few clients, hold off. There will be plenty of time to level up branding and marketing efforts as you grow.

- **Employees.** A series of independent contractors might suffice, Gerber says. The trick is weighing when you can financially support a full-time salaried employee—and when your continued growth (and sanity) depend on it.

- **Business consultants.** It's your job to learn what does and doesn't work, often by trial and error. "When you're first starting up, most times hiring a third-party consultant to educate you or tell you what you should be doing is not a worthwhile cost," Gerber says. "If they are not getting you in front of people, if they are not selling for you, they are not helping you."
- **Paid advisors.** "Don't confuse mentorship with partnership," Gerber explains. "Real advisors—people who are truly giving back—should not require equity or compensation at any time."

That's what teen entrepreneur Sam Gold did when he launched Yumvelope, a monthly snack-box subscription service that he ran until he left for college. Sales for Yumvelope more than doubled in the three years Gold ran it prior to shuttering the site. In college, he became a project manager for Stanford-funded ShoMe, which enables content creators to tell multimedia-enabled stories.

To keep costs down while growing his customer base, the Libertyville, Illinois entrepreneur spent eight months selling his care packages for foodies through Memberly, an online platform for subscription businesses that charged 5 percent of his sales.

"When you're just starting a business, to go with one of those plug-and-play tools is great," Gold says. "I didn't need all the bells and whistles of a custom website when I had no customers."

Three months into the venture, Gold had enough subscribers to warrant hiring a web designer. As an added bonus, he says, "I was able to go to that firm with a really clear idea of the functionality and design I wanted."

Budget was still a concern, though. Gold first tried to find a designer through the freelance marketplaces Elance-oDesk (now Upwork). Unfortunately, the quality of work wasn't up to snuff.

"Although I was paying rock-bottom rates, I wasn't getting any results," Gold says. That's when he bit the bullet and hired a web design firm referred by another subscription retail business. At several thousand dollars, creating the site "wasn't cheap," Gold says. "But I ended up with a tool that helped me convert customers quickly and efficiently."

The Beauty of Bartering

Bartering as an economic activity may date back into prehistory, but even today it's a thrifty way to snag the products and services your young business needs. However, sometimes it sounds easier in theory than it is in practice.

Take It from the Barter Kings

When money's tight, how can you grow your business? Trade for the items you need, say trading professionals and the hosts of A&E's 2012–2014 original trading show *Barter Kings*. Traders Steve McHugh and Antonio Palazzola have their own approach to trading up to get what they want—on the premier episode, the pair worked their way up in a series of six trades from a framed gold Elvis record to a powerboat.

While we might not all have the skill to trade up for more valuable items, barter is definitely a useful tool for business owners looking to stretch their budget. Freelance writers often trade writing for website design work and marketing consultations, for instance. In this tough economy, barter has boomed, and online barter exchanges that help you find items to barter for are mushrooming.

How can entrepreneurs barter for what they want without spending a dime, even if they don't have an item of equal value to trade? Here are seven tips from McHugh and Palazzola:

1. *Don't bring cash.* Palazzola has a strict policy of leaving his wallet at home when he goes to a trade. That way, when a trader wants to "even out" a trade by having you add in a few hundred dollars in cash, you can simply say you have no cash available. It's a straight trade or nothing.

2. *Look for the soft spot.* The pair chat up traders to find out why they're selling. For instance, one trader needed to get rid of his son's dirt bike because the boy had broken his leg, and his wife was mad. Another had made a vow to his wife not to ride motorcycles as long as they

had kids at home, so the bike had to go. When you know the trader has to ditch their item, you're in a stronger position to negotiate and trade them a slightly less valuable item.

3. *Be stoic.* Never let a trader see you're crazy hot to get an item. Stay impassive and act like you don't care to make the best deal.

4. *Leave some mystery.* When you're listing an item to trade, don't advertise all the details. Post a good photo and leave it with a basic description so the prospect has to call you to find out more.

5. *Craigslist rules.* Both hosts recommend the popular site as the top place to scan for trades. Not everyone posting on there will be savvy about how much their item is really worth, giving you an opening to potentially trade an item.

6. *Know your item's value.* You can't come out on top in a deal if you're not sure what both the item you're trading and the one you're getting are really worth. Often, traders will price items with sentimental value in mind or still have the original retail price in their heads, both of which are irrelevant to the resale market. Bring an experienced trader with you, or have a smartphone handy for checking eBay to establish what this item is selling for today in its current condition.

7. *Watch out for scams.* There are plenty of shady traders out there, Palazzola says. If you smell something fishy, run the other way.

A Bartering Fish Story: Q&A with Mack Chaffin, Co-Owner of The Elfish Company

What if the product you bring to the table is wild Alaska salmon, halibut, and lingcod? How do you find a web designer who's willing to take payment in fish?

This was the issue faced by Mack Chaffin, co-owner with his wife, Diane, of The Elfish Company, a fish distributor. Although he did a decent business selling fish through his website, at farmers markets, and to a handful of restaurants and grocery stores, Chaffin wanted to expand. (Chaffin has since moved on to other ventures, but his experience with bartering and Elfish remains instructive to this day.)

But marketing requires capital that the Dewey, Arizona–based businessman didn't have. So, at the end of 2011, when he discovered The

Barter Group, a trade exchange of 450 small businesses in Greater Phoenix, he leaped at the chance to join. *Entrepreneur* cast a line to Chaffin to find out more, and the following is an excerpt from that interview.

Entrepreneur: Why join a bartering organization?

Chaffin: Until now, the farmers market in Phoenix has been my primary source of revenue. I've been looking for ways to expand, to get the word out that we're here. But we don't have the kind of capital needed for advertising. Most of our capital has been used to purchase the freezers where we store our fish and other items to get the business established.

With the current economy, we can't exactly go to a bank for a loan. They're looking for somebody who's been in business a whole lot longer and has collateral. So when I learned about The Barter Group, it was perfect. You don't have to make a huge capital outlay every time you need services. You just swap something.

Entrepreneur: How does the group work?

Chaffin: When an individual wants to purchase some fish from us, what I get in return are "barter dollars," which are kept in my Barter Group "bank account." And then when I need to purchase a product or service, that credit will be there for me to use. It's much easier to do this than having to purchase the fish and still come up with other capital to pay a marketing company for their services.

Entrepreneur: What are the fees involved?

Chaffin: The Barter Group charges 6 percent cash on each transaction as well as a monthly maintenance fee of $10 in cash and $10 in trade. We were lucky enough to get a free membership last year due to a promotion going on when we joined.

Entrepreneur: What services do you plan to barter for?

Chaffin: Next year, we plan to spend $10,000 to $12,000 in barter dollars. We're hoping to do web design, branding, printing, promotional items like

T-shirts and hats, print and radio advertising, and strategic marketing, and to expand our social media reach.

It's almost tripling what our marketing budget was before. All you're spending is inventory. If we were to spend $12,000 on marketing, we'd be taking that in cash out of our pocket.

Entrepreneur: Why not just barter with other businesses on your own?

Chaffin: Going through The Barter Group is much easier than calling somebody out of the phone book and saying, "I need you to do this, and by the way, would you like to take some salmon as partial payment?" You don't know whether that would insult them, or they don't like fish, or they just don't want to barter.

Be Aware of Labor and Tax Rules

When Rebeca Mojica, owner and "creative guru" of Chicago jewelry company Blue Buddha Boutique, announced on Facebook that her shop was moving in 2011, customers responded, "How can we help?" and "I love to pack boxes!" That enthusiasm led her to "hire" three customers to help staff a booth at a craft show. The customers could opt to receive an hourly wage or be paid the equivalent of time-and-a-half in jewelry and supplies. All of them went for the latter, saving her $800—the difference between what it would have cost her to hire them at an hourly wage and the cost of materials to make the jewelry.

Smart Swapping

To find a bartering organization, begin with the websites of the National Association of Trade Exchanges (NATE; www.natebarter.com) and the International Reciprocal Trade Association (IRTA; www.irta.com)—both hold their members to strict ethical standards. Then try these tips from NATE board of directors member and past president Gary Oshry:

- **Assess the members.** Are the goods and services you need well represented? Are the businesses established, reputable, and located somewhere that's convenient for you?
- **Check references.** What do current members of the barter organization have to say? How about their local chamber of commerce or Better Business Bureau? Look online to see if there have been complaints.
- **Crunch the numbers.** Most bartering groups charge a onetime membership fee of up to $500 and a small monthly fee; some also charge an annual renewal fee. Many take a 10 to 15 percent commission on transactions.

"It's not a huge number, but for a four-day show, with a total booth staff of six, it makes a difference to my small business bottom line," says Mojica, who at the time planned to staff her shows and social media outreach efforts using volunteers, hoping to result in a savings of $250 to $300 per month. Since then, Blue Buddha has gone full-Etsy, with Mojica ultimately closing her shop and focusing all of her efforts on an Etsy venture.

While it's not unusual for small businesses to have friends or even enthusiastic customers who do what they can to see the business succeed, it's important to ensure that you don't inadvertently fall out of compliance with labor laws, says labor and employment attorney Truth Fisher of Advisors Law Group in Miami. In general, under the Fair Labor Standards Act (FLSA), individuals cannot volunteer services to for-profit, private-sector companies unless the activity benefits the employee, such as in the case of an unpaid internship. However, even such internships must pass strict Department of Labor criteria, Fisher says.

According to the U.S. Department of Labor, a company with annual revenue of less than $500,000 is exempt from FLSA requirements. In addition, unless the product is related to providing room and board, it is not a wage and is not subject to federal payroll taxes. States may differ in their interpretations, however. Fisher says the value of the product used as compensation should be at least the number of hours worked times minimum wage. Also, the employer may be liable for any injuries that the individual sustains while working.

"We advise all of our clients doing this," she says, "to have these employees covered by workers' compensation insurance."

Bootstrapping for the Long Haul: Making It Your Philosophy

Anyone who's started a business on a shoestring is adept at bootstrapping, or stretching resources—both financial and otherwise—as far as they can. Bootstrapping doesn't have to stop the second you get your first financing help. It's one of the most effective and inexpensive ways to ensure a business's positive cash flow. Bootstrapping means less money has to be borrowed and interest costs are reduced.

Trade Credit

Trade credit is one way to maximize your financial resources for the short term. Normally, suppliers extend credit to regular customers for 30, 60, or 90 days, without charging interest. However, when you first start your business, suppliers will want every order COD (cash or check on delivery) until you've established that you can pay your bills on time. While this is a fairly normal practice, in order to raise money during startup, you're going to have to try to negotiate a trade credit basis with suppliers. One of the things that will help you in these negotiations is having a written financial plan.

But using trade credit on a continual basis is not a long-term solution. Your business may become heavily committed to those suppliers who accept extended credit terms. As a result, you may no longer have ready access to other, more competitive suppliers who might offer lower prices, a superior product, and/or more reliable deliveries.

Depending on the terms available from your suppliers, the cost of trade credit can be quite high. For example, say you make a purchase from a supplier who decides to extend credit to you. The terms are a 2 percent cash discount within 10 days and a net date of 30 days. Essentially, the supplier is saying that if you pay within 10 days, the purchase price will be discounted by 2 percent. On the other hand, by forfeiting the 2 percent discount, you're able to use your money for 20 more days.

Factoring

Factoring is another way to stretch your money. It involves selling your receivables—money customers owe you—to a buyer, such as a commercial finance company, to raise capital. This is very common in industries such as the clothing industry, where long receivables are part of the business cycle. "Factors"—the factoring company you are selling to—usually buy accounts receivable at a rate that ranges between 75 and 90 percent of face value, and then add a discount rate of between 2 and 6 percent. For example, if the factoring company buys $20,000 worth of receivables and agrees to advance 90 percent of the total payment, then you will receive $18,000 (not taking a discount rate into account). The factor assumes the risk, and the task, of collecting the receivables. If your prices are set up to take factoring into account, you can still make a profit.

Other Credit

Customers can also help you obtain financing by writing you a letter of credit. For example, suppose you're starting a business manufacturing industrial bags, and a large corporation has placed an order for a steady supply of cloth bags. The major supplier that you'll source the material through is located in India. In this scenario, you obtain a letter of credit from your customer when the order is placed, and the material for the bags is purchased using this letter of credit as security.

If your business needs to buy its facility, your initial costs may be high, but the building's cost can be financed over a long-term period of 15 to 30 years. The loan on the facility can be structured to make optimum use of your planned growth or seasonal peaks. For instance, you can arrange a graduated payment mortgage that initially has very small monthly payments, with the cost increasing over the lifetime of the loan. The lower initial monthly payments give your business time to grow. Eventually, you can refinance the loan when time and interest rates permit.

Another advantage is that real estate appreciates over time and creates a valuable asset called equity. You can borrow against this equity—lenders often loan up to 75 or 80 percent of a property's appraised value. This also applies to any personal real estate you own. Home equity loans are a popular financing device for new business owners because there's often substantial equity tied up in a home, and the loans are easy to come by.

If you spend a lot of money on equipment, you may find yourself without enough working capital to keep your business going in its first months. Instead of paying cash for your equipment, the manufacturer can effectively loan you the money by selling you the equipment on an installment basis. This helps conserve your working capital while allowing you to use the equipment in the meantime.

Two types of credit contracts are commonly used to finance equipment purchases:

1. *The conditional sales contract.* The purchaser doesn't receive title to the equipment until it's fully paid for.
2. *The chattel-mortgage contract.* The equipment becomes the property of the purchaser on delivery, but the seller holds a mortgage claim against it until the amount specified in the contract is paid.

Leasing

Leasing is another way to avoid financing the outright purchase of high-ticket items like equipment, vehicles, furniture, and computers. With leasing, you pay for only that portion you use, rather than for the entire purchase price. When you're just starting out in business, it might make sense to shop around and get the best leasing arrangement possible. For example, you could lease a photocopier for several hundred dollars a month rather than financing the entire $3,000 purchase price, or you could lease your automobile or van instead of shelling out $25,000 or more for the full purchase price of the car.

There are many ways a lease can be modified to increase your cash position:

▷ A down payment lower than 10 percent, or no down payment at all.
▷ Maintenance costs that are built into the lease package, thereby reducing your cash outlays. If you needed to pay employees or a repairperson to do maintenance on purchased equipment, it could wind up costing you more than if you had leased it.

⟩ Extending the lease term to cover the entire life of the property (or use of the property for as long as you wish).

⟩ A purchase option that allows you to buy the property after the lease period has ended. A fixed purchase price can also be added to the option provision.

⟩ Lease payments that can be structured to accommodate seasonal variations in the business or tied to indexes that track interest to create an adjustable lease.

Bootstrap financing really begins and ends with your attention to careful management of your financial resources. Be aware of what you spend and keep your overhead low. If you need to go the top-dollar route, make sure you can justify the expense. Don't choose an overly expensive office or location unless it's really going to pay off in increased sales. Take a look at secondhand furniture—if it works for your office, buy it. Barter for goods and services when appropriate. Buy on promotion to take advantage of better prices offered for a limited time.

Keep a close watch on operating expenses. If interest rates are high, it won't take too many unpaid bills to wipe out your profits. At a 12 percent interest rate, carrying an unpaid $10,000 in bills will cost you $120 per month. Tight margins mean it's costlier to accumulate bills than increase production.

CHAPTER 3

Using Traditional Lending Institutions

The traditional way to get a business loan was to approach your favorite local bank with a business plan and secure the financing right then and there. Although several other avenues exist to obtain the financial backing to launch your business—from crowdfunding to grants—the bank-loan approach is still viable and may work well for some businesses.

The chances of securing a bank loan hang on various factors, including the general economic climate, government regulations, and the bank's lending policies. Learning some tips and tricks can help boost your odds of securing a loan. So let's explore this time-honored route of getting your hands on some cash to finance your business.

Watch Out for These Costly Traps

Although the lure of quick cash can be tempting, be wary of common traps when considering a lender for your company:

▷ *Know when business credit services are necessary—and when they absolutely are not.* While business credit can be important as your business matures, it doesn't make a difference for a startup applying for a loan. Startups are not expected to have a strong business credit file, so beware any firm extolling the necessity of business credit services to apply for a loan. Instead, concentrate on the strength of your personal credit.

▷ *Know the price of speed and convenience.* Some short-term lenders and cash advance companies offer so-called "fast" loans with quick application processes and a lax review of personal credit. This speed and convenience come at a cost. Be careful when considering a cash advance, especially if rates and payoff time frames are harsh. Some firms offer annualized percentage rates as high as 200 percent with amortizations as slow as three to four months. Read all terms carefully.

▷ *Know your own business plan.* Be wary of any company insisting that you need a business plan and financial forecast, and then trying to sell you an expensive business plan package. And if you're paying someone else to do this work for you, your business may have bigger problems. Having a direct hand in developing your business plan and financial projections ensures that you, the business owner, know the ins and outs of your company and have defined goals for growth.

Busting Myths about Small Business Lending

With the growing accessibility of information online, modern entrepreneurs in search of funding to grow their businesses have a huge leg up on generations past. Yet for every bit of accurate and genuinely helpful advice, there is an increasing amount of misinformation and myths surrounding the small business lending space. Unfortunately, much of that misinformation can give business owners a false sense of their own eligibility for small business loans.

Don't miss out on opportunities to secure funding for your business due to false information. Let's separate fact from fiction and bust five of the most common small business lending myths we hear every day.

Myth 1: Approval Takes Forever

Whether you're itching to move forward with a new business idea or need cash quickly to cover an unexpected expense, one of the most common questions business owners have when applying for funding is, "How fast can I get cash in hand?"

You may hear from well-meaning friends and relatives that getting approved for a business loan can take weeks or even months, but that information is outdated. With new online loan applications, an organized business owner can complete their application in less than an hour, and it can be reviewed and approved within 24 hours of submission. Many lenders can even offer cash in hand in as little as two days.

While some borrowers may take additional time to gather financial statements or get their credit reports in better shape, once you hit "submit," the approval practice is very efficient. Don't let the fear of a long approval process hold you back from seeking a loan.

Myth 2: New Businesses Never Qualify

The startup funding quandary is a difficult one. You need an established business to secure funding, but you need cash in hand to get your business off the ground. Seeking funding from venture capitalists or angel investors is a popular route for securing startup funding (see Chapter 9), but is it the only way?

Many startup entrepreneurs assume they need to be in business for a few years and have established business credit before they can qualify for a loan. However, more and more lenders are specifically offering startup loans that require little or no business credit history to qualify.

Applying for a startup loan will involve more scrutiny into your personal finances than other types of business loans. Your personal credit score will be the most important part of the application. You may also be faced with less favorable rates than you would receive as an established business. But if you're committed to finding funding and open to the necessary conditions, securing a loan for your brand-new business is possible.

Myth 3: Online Lenders Are Con Artists with Unreasonable Rates

We get it. The online alternative lending market is relatively new, and people are skeptical of new things. Unfortunately, many unscrupulous online lenders and brokers have engaged in predatory and dangerous lending practices, giving the entire industry a bad rap.

But in reality, some alternative lenders operating online offer single-digit interest rates. Those offering higher rates are often working with borrowers who are considered risky. Online lenders regularly consider a wide variety of borrower credentials aside from just the traditional credit report and score. Business owners who were turned down by their bank can frequently find the funding they need online. See Chapter 8 for more on this possibility.

As with any financial transaction, it's critical that business owners do their due diligence about an online lender before signing on the dotted line.

Myth 4: Loan Officers Only Care about Your Credit Score

This myth, carried over from the outdated traditional bank model for loan approvals, can leave business owners with less-than-stellar credit feeling hopeless about their funding prospects. Luckily for these entrepreneurs, growth in the alternative lending sector has led to a larger spectrum of factors being considered in the loan approval process.

Many lenders will now give equal weight to your company's revenue history, cash flow statement, and other financial documents in determining your loan eligibility. This information often paints a very different picture of a business and its owner's financial standing than what a credit score alone can convey.

Even so, before applying for a business loan, it is still important to take steps to make your credit report and score the best possible reflection of your financial history. Always make debt payments on time and manage your credit usage responsibly. Also frequently check your credit reports for accuracy. If you find errors, contact the reporting agencies to correct the mistakes.

Myth 5: Approval Is Determined by a Heartless Algorithm

Once upon a time, entrepreneurs seeking small business funding could walk into their local community bank, build face-to-face relationships with managers and loan officers, and be confident they understood the whole picture behind their loan application, including the cold, hard numbers as well as the more intangible elements of their qualifications as borrowers.

These days, technology has all but replaced those in-person banking relationships, creating the impression that loan approval decisions are controlled by nothing more than a few concrete variables and an algorithm saying "yes" or "no."

In reality, lenders consider a wide variety of objective, number-based factors as well as more subjective considerations, like your business and marketing plan.

If you're concerned about certain elements of your loan application, like your credit score, take the time to flesh out your business plan, fully explaining how the funds you are borrowing will be used and how this investment will lead to a successful business. You'll read more about credit scores later in this chapter.

Ultimately, your lender's main consideration is whether you will make your loan payments on time, every time. Your loan application should, both through financial documents and through your written statements, paint the best possible picture of your future ability to repay the loan. Here are three areas small business owners need to focus on when they apply to obtain credit:

▷ *Show that your business generates steady cash flow.* Cash flow is a key indicator of a business's health and its future prospects. When you can show reliable cash flow for your business, your lender can see that you have the resources to pay for new loans.

▷ *Make sure your current debt load is manageable.* Your lender wants to make sure your business can take on additional debt and still manage its debt payments. Lenders may also look at a business owner's household and personal debt.

▷ *Maintain a good payment history.* Before extending credit, a lender needs to be confident that a business has the ability to repay. Your payment history provides an important record of your ability to responsibly pay down debt. That's why obtaining and using a credit card responsibly for everyday business expenses can be a good way to begin building a payment history for your business.

If you do your research, stay organized, and clearly and concisely convey this information to lenders on your loan application, your chances of being quickly matched with a loan will tremendously improve.

The Business Credit Score

No one ever promised that the challenges to growing a small business would be minor. Entrepreneurs regularly confront issues that can threaten the very core of their companies, not the least of which is difficulty securing the financing they need to run and grow a sustainable business.

Finding capital is becoming harder for a significant proportion of small businesses, despite the wider variety of financing options available. Even though there are more lending alternatives for small businesses than ever before, a crucial step is missing and no one is paying attention, leaving business owners increasingly frustrated over their rejections for credit lines and loans.

The dream and the reality don't add up—a scenario confirmed by a 2015 Nav survey of 250 small and midsize business owners, which brings to light the struggle around bank financing, small-business loans, and the rejections small businesses suffer.

The Realities Small Businesses Face

The Small Business American Dream Gap Report found that despite the positive outlook for small businesses, nearly three out of ten small businesses reported finding it harder than in the past to reduce operating costs. Nearly a quarter of small businesses, meanwhile, found it harder to plan for unforeseen expenses. Within the previous year, the survey revealed, 20 percent of the small businesses surveyed said they had considered shutting down, primarily because of lack of growth or cash flow issues.

Those kinds of struggles had led 53 percent of those small businesses to apply for funding or credit lines over the past five years—and one in four said they had sought loans multiple times. Yet 20 percent of those applying over the past 60 months reported being turned down, and 45 percent of those denied said they'd been rejected more than once. The most frustrating finding was that nearly a fourth—23 percent—of these businesses didn't know why they'd been denied.

As a result, 26 percent of these business owners avoided hiring and expansion because they were frustrated with trying to access funds. Instead, they ponied up the money from their personal savings and used their credit cards to cover expenses and keep their businesses going, putting them at substantial risk.

In addition, the study determined that the last time the owners surveyed had needed funds, 62 percent had withdrawn personal savings, 22 percent had used business credit cards, 24 percent had used their personal credit cards, and 10 percent had relied on family and friends. Only 36 percent of those seeking funds had obtained bank loans.

Your Business Credit Score Is the Crucial Missing Link

The study revealed that a primary reason why small businesses can't obtain bank loans is their failure to understand their business credit score. Some 45 percent of entrepreneurs surveyed didn't even know they had a business credit score, and 72 percent didn't know where to find information about it. Even when they did, more than eight in ten small business owners surveyed acknowledged that they didn't know how to interpret their score.

Education and empowerment around creditworthiness is a core issue that can make or break a small business's ability to get financing. Many business owners starting out are unaware of business credit and may do significant damage to their credit without realizing it—primarily by maxing out personal credit cards and/or credit lines because they believe they have no other choice. This short-term approach can lead to significant long-term damage.

Unsure whether your business appears as a credit risk? Consider the FICO score. Just as every individual consumer has one based on his or her personal credit record, every business has one developed by the FICO LiquidCredit Small Business Scoring Service—the FICO SBSS score. Banks use this score to evaluate term loans and lines of credit up to $1 million.

Like your business credit score—determined by factors such as payment history, credit utilization, and public records—your SBSS score will impact your likelihood of securing business loans; however, your SBSS score and your business credit score are used by different entities to evaluate the level of credit risk your business represents.

The SBSS score rank-orders small businesses by their likelihood of making on-time payments based on their personal and business credit history, along with other financial data. On a scale of 0 to 300, a small business must score at least 140 to pass the pre-screening process the SBA uses for its most popular loan—the 7(a) loan.

If a business with a poor credit history—or none at all—is denied financing, lenders are not required to notify the owner of the reason for the rejection. It's crucial, therefore, for business owners to learn about their SBSS score and build credit with timely payments to vendors and suppliers to keep that score up. Boosting their score may take years for companies with a poor or nonexistent credit history, so the process of strengthening creditworthiness needs to begin long before they submit a credit application.

A number of business credit bureaus will generate a business credit score, including Dun & Bradstreet, Equifax, Experian, and FICO. Anyone can request a business credit report from Dun & Bradstreet, Equifax, or Experian, but it comes at a price. Nav offers a free service that provides access to summary reports from Dun & Bradstreet and Experian, a personal TransUnion report, and alerts associated with any changes to business or personal credit.

Until recently, there was no direct way to access your FICO SBSS score, but small businesses can now get that number through Nav's subscription service. It's the only place small businesses can get that score online.

Why All This Matters

Ultimately, those who understand business credit are better positioned to succeed. The Nav study found that nearly 40 percent of small business owners who didn't know their business credit score anticipated growth of less than 5 percent, while the nearly three-quarters who did know it envisioned growth of up to 20 percent.

Another answer to the perplexity surrounding rejected funding came from a revelation in the study about owners' understanding of credit issues. The small business owners surveyed who understood their business credit scores, the study reported, were 41 percent more likely to be approved for a business loan than those who did not. And they were 31 percent more likely to consider expanding their businesses.

Some 80 percent of those in the know about their scores, moreover, considered their funding process to have been smooth, and half of those owners indicated they were less likely to turn to personal savings to grow their companies.

Business owners, then, should determine where they stand and take control of the factors critical to the lenders, credit card companies, and even other businesses they work with. When owners understand their scores, they have an easier loan approval experience and are empowered to grow and thrive and help the overall economy thrive as well. That way, everyone wins.

10 Questions to Ask before Applying for a Bank Loan

Applying for a bank loan involves much more than filling out paperwork and saying a prayer. Among other things, you need to consider the state of your personal and business finances, how you're going to repay the loan, and how much money you actually need. This section talks about some of the key questions you should ask before starting an application.

Is It Likely I Will Qualify for the Loan?

You're only going to hurt your credit if you apply for a loan you won't get. "Just like if you get declined for a personal credit card, it makes it more difficult to borrow in the future," says David Gass, a business consultant and CEO of Anderson Business Advisors. "If you get turned down, it looks to the next bank like you're a bad risk." He suggests asking lending institutions about their specific requirements before applying. Many will let you know the minimum credit score they require, the cash flow you need to show, and other qualifying factors.

How Much Do I Really Need?

Before you approach the bank, make sure you have a good handle on how much cash you actually need. Startup costs for a business is a tally of all expenses that will be incurred while you are preparing to open for business, such as research expenses, borrowing costs, and investment in technology, as well as employee expenses and investment in advertising and promotion. Startup costs vary for different types of businesses, such as sole proprietorships or partnerships, so be sure you understand what the costs will be for your business.

Do I Have Adequate Cash Flow to Repay the Loan?

The best way to determine this is to create a monthly cash flow projection. Refer to the cash flow projection worksheet (Figure 1.1 on page 5).

For example, if your customer pays you in 60 days, but you have to pay your vendors in 15 days, you might need some extra money to tide you over. "It will reflect poorly on you if you come into the bank asking for $50,000, then they ask you to create a cash flow projection and you find out that you actually need $100,000," says Adam Hoeksema, cofounder of Indiana-based ProjectionHub, a web app to help entrepreneurs make financial projections. "You should know how much you need and how you will use the funds before approaching the bank." The worksheet in Figure 1.2 on pages 7–8 can help you determine how much cash your startup business may need.

Your banker will probably ask you to provide financial projections for the business. Make sure to include your debt repayment plan in those projections. Bankers are going to be looking for businesses that have some wiggle room, and you may need to show available cash flow that is three times greater than your debt payment requirements, Hoeksema says. "They don't want to see if you lose one customer, you won't be able to make your loan payment this month," he says. "If your projections show that you have very little room for error, you are likely to scare them away."

How Much Can I Borrow Based on the Asset I'm Using for Collateral?

Business owners often think if they purchase a piece of equipment for $100,000, they should be able to borrow $100,000 by pledging the equipment as collateral. But banks usually don't agree, Hoeksema says. "Banks will value your asset below what you think the value should be, and then they will only lend up to a certain percentage of the value of the asset." For example, banks might lend up to 70 percent of the value of a new piece of equipment, and maybe only 60 percent for used equipment.

Will the Money Help My Business Grow?

If you're borrowing $10,000 for payroll or other routine operating expenses, you're not generating more revenue from the loan and could find yourself in the same spot three to six months from now. Instead, you should put borrowed dollars into the parts of the business that will generate more revenue over time and help reduce future borrowing needs, Gass says. "If I take that dollar and leverage it, put it into sales and marketing, and drive more revenues—$1 driving $5—then it's worth it. It's all about growing the business."

How Good Is My Business Credit Score?

As discussed in the previous section, many people may know their personal credit score, but very few know their business score, says Rohit Arora, CEO and cofounder of Biz2Credit, a New York City–based company that arranges loans for small businesses. As with personal credit, you can find your business credit score through Experian, TransUnion, or Equifax. If the score isn't as high as you think it should be, it might be because there are outstanding liens against your business. Also check to make sure your vendors are reporting your payments. You can try to boost your score by reducing the balance on your business credit cards or requesting a credit-line increase to lower the percentage of your available credit in use. "The lender is going to check your business, and your score is the final arbiter of whether you get the loan or not," Arora says. "Even if you have stellar personal credit and good assets, if a lot of business contacts are saying you're paying them late, that's going to scare off lenders."

Are My Personal Finances in Order?

Bankers may want to look at your "global financial statement," including personal information like outstanding student loans, personal credit card debt, and mortgage payments. Until your business reaches a substantial size ($5 million to $10 million in annual revenue or more), the bank is going to rely heavily on your personal financial statement and personal credit score to determine the creditworthiness of your business. "If you have a $200,000 mortgage on a house worth $250,000, and you have $200,000 in student loans, the bank may not see you as a good candidate for a loan," Hoeksema says. "If you have a lot of personal debt and very little collateral that you can provide to the bank, you may need to find a strong co-signer."

Do I Have All the Documentation I Need to Apply for the Loan?

Arora says some studies have shown that as many as four in five loans never close—"not because the business didn't qualify, but because of the paper chase." When applying for a business loan, you will need a lot of documentation. For example, if you're seeking an SBA loan, Arora recommends you provide the last three years of business and personal tax returns, personal financial statements, and financial projections for the next 12 to 24 months. "If you go to the [lender] and are not fully prepared, not only does it make you look unprofessional, but by the time you get the documentation in place, it might be outdated," he says.

Does the Loan Have a Prepayment Penalty?

When taking out a loan, find out if you're free to pay it off early without any penalty. Some states allow lenders to charge prepayment penalties, in which case you should try to negotiate a compromise. For example, you could agree to a penalty only if you pay off the loan in a relatively short period of time, say, within six months from the time of the loan. "Prepayment is especially valuable if you believe your business may grow soon, and you may need a larger line of credit," says Jeanne Brutman, a New York City–based financial planner for small business owners. "By having good excess cash and a paid-off or [paid-down] line of credit, it shows the lender you are responsible with debt and can handle an increase in your total credit."

If I Die, How Will the Loan Be Repaid?

It's something most people don't like to think about, but in the event of your death, an unpaid business loan can affect your family. "Most people think, if I die, the bank is out of luck, but that's not true," Brutman says. If you leave a large life insurance policy, for example, the bank may come after that. Find out what a lender's policy is in the event of your death to best determine how to protect your family. "Most business owners understand that if they're collateralizing their house and the business fails, they could lose their house," Brutman says. "But they may not understand that if they die, it doesn't cancel out their debts." It may be best to put your assets in your spouse's name, if the spouse doesn't have an ownership stake in the business. Brutman also recommends personal property and casualty insurance coverage, which, in the event of your death, takes business debt into consideration.

Qualifying for an SBA Loan: Remember the Five Cs

If you plan to start or expand a business, chances are you'll need to seek funding. In a 2015 study by Bank of America, 24 percent of entrepreneurs indicated they intended to seek a business loan within the coming year. Many of those would apply for an SBA loan through an approved lender.

When applying for an SBA loan, consider a group commonly known as the 5 Cs: five factors that banks analyze to determine whether to approve your small business loan application. Guidant Financial is one company that works with entrepreneurs on those 5 Cs every day to help them obtain an SBA loan. Here's a look at the factors Guidant has found to be important to banks, particularly when it comes to SBA loan qualifiers.

Capital

Also referred to in the industry as *equity injection*, capital is your skin in the game in the lending transaction. No bank will fund your business at 100 percent of your total cash needs. If you're creating a new business, typically the bank will require you to contribute 30 percent. If you're acquiring an existing business, expect your contribution to be 20 percent.

Capital is a deal-breaker for banks. Most advisors will tell you not to proceed with preparing a loan application if you cannot provide the required contribution.

If you don't have the capital, your goal becomes to figure out how to raise it: find a business partner, use a rollover for business startup arrangement, or cash out an investment. Note that you may not use borrowed money as an equity injection. Don't, for example, go looking for a home equity line of credit as your capital investment. If a bank discovers that your capital contribution is subject to debt service, it will likely deny your loan.

Credit

Credit comprises your personal credit score, your credit history, and an analysis of your credit utilization. A new trend in SBA lending is that banks may also use the FICO SBSS to assess your credit risk. If you can't meet the minimum scores (which vary among lenders), you'll need to step back and take the time to improve your credit score and your credit presence.

It's better to do your homework up front. You can receive one free credit report per year from each of the big three credit reporting agencies mentioned in the previous section (and in our resource list at the end of this book). Check each for accuracy and consistency, and take care of any issues that might be a red flag for the bank.

Capacity

To reiterate, capacity, or cash flow, represents your ability to generate income that will pay your debts. If you're starting a new business, the bank assesses your global cash flow—your current personal income as well as your projected income from the business. If you're acquiring an existing company, the lender wants to see that the last three years of business tax returns reflect positive cash flow and profit.

The bank won't give you money if it sees no evidence that you can repay it. Your capacity is an important part of the evaluation process for the loan. If you don't have sufficient capacity, consider bringing on a partner to add cash flow to the scenario.

Character

Character isn't a question of your personal charm—it's your business character the bank will assess. What's your business experience in general, and in the industry in which your new business will operate? Have you managed profits and losses successfully in your previous business or for an employer? Have you worked your way up through an industry and gained experience in multiple aspects of its operations?

Your SBA loan application should draw from the same work you do when preparing your business plan—mapping your experience to the skills necessary to run your business.

The SBA does care about some aspects of your personal history as well. Would-be borrowers are often surprised to learn that they must provide information on any current criminal charges they are subject to, any recent arrests on charges, any convictions or guilty pleas in their history, and, if they are at least a 50 percent owner in the applicant business, whether they are delinquent on child support.

Collateral

Entrepreneurs can also be badly caught off guard by the SBA's stance on collateral. The SBA expects its loans to be fully secured, but it will not generally decline a loan based on inadequate collateral, assuming the borrower satisfies the other four standards. However, if you have what the SBA terms "worthwhile assets," the lending bank will require they be used as security for the loan.

In particular, if you own a home with a value of greater than 20 percent equity, the bank will take a lien against your home as security for the business loan, whereas if you don't own a home and meet all other loan criteria, the bank will likely approve your loan unsecured. It can be unpleasant for entrepreneurs with a more solid financial base to discover that they are required to take on more personal risk than some of their peers.

This can particularly bring business partners into conflict with each other if one has a qualifying equity stake in a home and the other does not, since the home-owning partner will be required to assume this risk to proceed with the loan application.

What are nonnegotiable qualifications to obtain an SBA loan? Banks are looking for personal credit ratings in the high 600s and up. Recent bankruptcies or no evidence of cash flow are also generally deal-breakers.

Entrepreneurs should remember every bank or lender interprets the SBA regulations a little differently. If you are turned down by one lender but believe you have a strong business case, keep searching.

As always, consult a financial professional before entering the application process. Experts can save you time and frustration by helping you understand (and, if necessary, improve) your position. Guidant counsels entrepreneurs to have their accounting in order and then make sure they're aligning themselves with the right partners who want to help them succeed—and who aren't sticking them in a trap of unfavorable loans with interest rates that can cripple their business right out of the gate.

The 5 Cs aren't just barriers to overcome. They are the path to bankability. When the 5 Cs align for the bank, there's a much better chance they'll align for the success of your business as well.

You can find out more about SBA loan programs at the SBA website: www.sba.gov/category/lender-navigation/sba-loan-programs.

Buying a Business through Seller Financing

Often seller financing loans, in which the seller "lends" the buyer a percentage of the sale price, involve the SBA.

Advertising and publishing veteran Janelle Regotti was looking for a business to buy. The right opportunity presented itself in 2014 when she found Guide Publishing (now called Archer Publishing, LCC), a company that distributed a quarterly resource guide for northeast Ohio seniors. The only catch: Regotti didn't have the $500,000 asking price.

With few physical assets to borrow against, she was unlikely to get a bank loan. So, with the help of her business broker, she negotiated a seller-financing deal and bought the business five months later with just 10 percent down and quarterly payments due over 10 years at about 6 percent interest.

Of course, most sellers won't finance 90 percent of their asking price. But borrowing 10, 20, or even 30 percent from a seller at a competitive rate still beats using your credit card to cover capital shortfalls. If you're interested in seller financing, here's what you need to know.

When It Makes Sense

Being short on cash isn't the only reason to push for seller financing; it is also a viable solution if the seller and potential buyer cannot agree on a price. With seller financing, the seller agrees to finance part of the purchase price, which bridges the gap between what the buyer is asking and what the seller is offering. To do this, the buyer and seller must negotiate the terms of the loan, such as the amount of the loan, the interest rate, the repayment period, and any collateral or security for the loan.

Renzo Aida went this route when he bought a dance studio near Boston in 2013. He had the money to pay the six-figure asking price in full but thought the seller wanted 20 percent too much.

"I wanted him to put his money where his mouth was," Aida says. Both parties went into negotiations and eventually got what they wanted. Aida has since increased revenue by 28 percent.

What Sellers Expect

Besides cashing out, sellers want assurances their baby will be in good hands. They want a buyer who has experience in the industry, a solid business plan, working capital, and roots in the community, says William White, regional developer of Murphy Business & Financial Corporation, a national business brokerage firm. Sellers treat these loans as seriously as any bank would, says White, who lives in Hudson, Ohio. This means requiring a credit check, collateral (business assets and possibly your home), and life insurance. Loan terms often extend up to ten years, interest rates are comparable with those offered by banks, and it's typical for sellers to stick around for 60 to 90 days post-sale to advise the buyers.

How to Vet the Deal

It's not enough to grill the owner on the intricacies of their business. You have to scour the financials, from bank statements and cash flow to tax returns and profit-and-loss (P&L) reports. You also have to inspect the physical property to ensure all inventory, equipment, and other assets are accounted for and in working order. "Otherwise, you don't know what you're getting," Regotti warns.

Trusting the seller is imperative. "Make sure it's someone you actually want to be in business with after the sale is complete," says Regotti, who negotiated a six-month transition period during which the seller played consultant. Another must: having a business attorney in your corner, even if you're working with a broker. "I had my attorney look over everything," she adds.

What to Negotiate

Owners may not openly advertise their willingness to partially finance a sale—but, according to White, it's common for them to consider lending at least 5 to 15 percent of the purchase price.

KC Truby of Tucson, Arizona, who has bought six owner-financed businesses over the past five decades, suggests agreeing to the asking price but getting creative on the terms. Regotti, for example, nabbed 90 percent seller financing by promising to apply for an SBA loan two years down the line. If she gets it, she'll pay off the seller in full. Other buyers can bridge valuation disagreements with an earn-out clause that grants the seller extra pay during a set period if profits meet or surpass expectations.

"You can dream up 100 different ways to do this," Truby explains. "It really boils down to what the owner wants to accomplish."

The Advantages of Seller Financing for Startups: Q&A with Bill Short, President and CEO, FiberTech

Bill Short wasn't worried about how he'd finance FiberTech, the Atlanta-area fiber optics company he wanted to purchase. The former banking professional had stellar credit and enough money to make a sizable down payment on the business, which was priced in the "low seven figures."

The rest, he imagined, he'd borrow. But when Short applied for an SBA loan, he was told the government body required at least 10 percent of the deal to be financed by the seller. Although Short hadn't considered taking a loan from the seller, he was happy to comply if the terms were right.

"Seller financing helps get the deal done," says Kent Reed of Murphy Business & Financial Corporation, the brokerage firm that worked with Short. "It helps the buyer with less out of pocket. And it gives them more confidence in the deal if the seller's got some skin in the game."

Short wound up making a 40 percent down payment on FiberTech, borrowing an additional 50 percent through an SBA loan, and borrowing the remaining 10 percent from the seller. "It helped me to not have to put in that additional 10 percent," Short says. With the extra cash, he was able to boost the company's marketing efforts, invest in vehicles and equipment, and ramp up staff from 14 to 20.

Since purchasing FiberTech in March 2011, Short has seen revenue increase by about 20 percent. *Entrepreneur* asked him for details of his seller financing deal, and the following section includes that exchange.

Entrepreneur: *Is the seller still involved with the business?*

Short: I bought 100 percent of the company from him, but he did agree to work as a consultant on an as-needed basis. For the most part, I haven't needed to engage him. But he still has a vested interest in the company until we pay off the note. That's one of the positives about seller financing: If a seller isn't willing to give you any financing, that might tell you something about what he thinks of the deal.

Entrepreneur: *Is it important to have a good rapport with the previous owner?*

Short: When you are introduced to somebody who is trying to sell a company, one of the first questions out of your mouth is always, "Why do you want to sell?" As you go through the due-diligence process, you pretty quickly figure out what's going on. At some point you have to ask, "Do I trust this person, or don't I?"

Entrepreneur: *What are your repayment terms?*

Short: It's basically a three-year, fixed-rate note. I make semiannual payments. Over three years, I'll pay him principal and 5.75 percent interest every six months.

Entrepreneur: *How did your broker help negotiate this deal?*

Short: The broker spoke with the seller to let him know that it was normal in a transaction of this size for the seller to take back some of the note. It wasn't like it just came out of the blue from me. So the seller was probably anticipating that might be part of the offer. Now, if I came back and said, "I need 80 percent financing because I can't get any bank financing," I doubt he would have taken the deal. There were other people interested in the company at the time. I was only asking for 10 percent of the deal, and he gets full payout in three years, so I think he thought that was reasonable.

Entrepreneur: **What advice would you offer to others interested in seller financing?**

Short: I strongly recommend that you have that conversation very early on to see if seller financing is an option. It really can make or break the deal. It might allow you to pay a little bit more for the company. For somebody who doesn't have access to a lot of capital, you could structure it so that if the company does well, the seller might even get a little bit of a scrape on the profits. Just don't make the note so short that you can't reasonably repay it. If you can't pay everything back, you might end up giving the company back.

Microfinancing Small Business

A small $10,000 to $50,000 loan from a microfinance organization may be a more realistic bet for an early-stage company than a sizable bank loan. Microfinance loans are small loans typically in the range of up to $50,000 in the United States, with an average loan amount between $9,000 and $10,000. Microloans started as a solution for impoverished borrowers in underdeveloped countries. These borrowers typically lacked collateral, steady employment, and a verifiable credit history, making them difficult candidates for traditional financing options. Microloans have been successful in helping to support entrepreneurship and encourage economic growth in these developing nations.

In more recent years, microlenders have been establishing themselves all across the United States. Some microlenders are finding creative ways to improve and streamline this already simple process by offering unique services. (For example, they often help lower-income and minority business owners and offer mentorship and education.)

How Microfinance Can Help Small Business

Nonbank lenders provide loans that average just $7,000. Here's the funny part: The businesses they lend to have a survival rate that's twice the national average. Repayment rates are on par with traditional banks, too.

Why do micro-borrowers do better than owners who use traditional bank loans or credit cards? Here are three reasons:

1. *Better vetting.* Microlenders tend to spend more time getting to know a business owner one-on-one, which usually doesn't happen at major banks. These microlending institutions often take bigger risks on unproven startups, but because they take the time to learn a lot about the person seeking the loan, they form a more personal connection. With those closer ties having been forged, entrepreneurs will go the extra mile to avoid disappointing the person who approved their loan.

2. *Support groups.* Most microloans are made in a group setting. The business owners in a lending circle support one another and, in some cases, are financially responsible for each other's loans. This web of interconnected responsibility helps keep them on track, provides moral support, and gives entrepreneurs another set of people they don't want to let down.

3. *Smaller loans.* When entrepreneurs only have a small sum on which to start their businesses, they watch every dime carefully. Too often, landing a big loan can lead to profligate spending rather than growth and productivity. Small borrowers also don't get delusions of global domination—they take it one careful step at a time, so they don't stumble into overexpansion.

Inside PayPal's Working Capital Program

If you're a big PayPal user, you may be able to take advantage of the company's Working Capital program, which allows businesses to borrow money flexibly. In lieu of fixed terms, the loan amount is repaid as a percentage of a business's PayPal sales. If sales taper off, for whatever reason, you aren't tied to an unrealistic repayment amount.

Unlike traditional loans, which often come with a variety of interest charges and fees, including early prepayment penalties, business owners are charged a single, fixed fee, based on the information PayPal has on their business. The loan is repaid faster if business is booming, and more slowly should it encounter unexpected obstacles.

"PayPal Working Capital flexes with the businesses' sales cycle," Norah Coelho, a senior director of Global Merchant Lending at PayPal, says, whether it's cyclical or seasonal. It also helps business owners manage through unexpected events, including health issues, family matters, or "any of the normal things that happen in a person's life." A minimum payment only needs to be made once every 90 days to stay in good standing. If a business is closed due to the owner's need to take care of family—PayPal Working Capital's flexibility allows the business to focus on what they need to focus on.

When you're running a business, time is a scarce resource: Dropping everything to go to the bank and fill out a lengthy application isn't always a realistic option.

The entire process of accessing financing through PayPal takes place online. Because potential borrowers are already PayPal customers, the company is able to pre-populate most of the application information. Once you submit the application, you'll receive an answer instantaneously. Given the company's knowledge of an applicant's PayPal sales history, "we do a real-time assessment," Coelho says. "There is no checking of a credit bureau, no calculating cash flow or coverage ratios. We are able to make an immediate decision."

If approved, customers can evaluate the fixed fee, determine if they want to borrow the entire amount offered, and decide the percentage of each sale they'll commit to repaying the loan (this ranges from 10 percent to 30 percent). Should they accept the terms, the money will be deposited in their PayPal account immediately. Altogether, the entire process only takes around five to ten minutes.

This speed and ease are important. "We hear from business owners who are busy from 9-to-5 selling, stocking, packing mailers with their products," Coelho says. "They may be parents taking care of children; they may have another full-time job." An intuitive, 24/7 online system means "a business owner who is a mom can apply for financing after the kids have been put to bed, or on a Sunday night when she has more bandwidth."

PayPal Working Capital takes a wealth of data into consideration, including the business' sales history with PayPal, rather than simply revenue or a business owner's credit score. This was the case when PayPal Working Capital approved a loan for a small chain of bakeries in New York City, despite the business having gone through a difficult period. A traditional institution wouldn't have reached the same decision. PayPal could see that the business had turned a corner. Sales were up; it was doing well. As a result, the business owner was approved for financing through PayPal, enabling him to move his flagship bakery and eventually open additional locations and create an opportunity for his business to thrive.

To apply, start by going to https://www.paypal.com/workingcapital/. Note that your business must have had a PayPal Business or Premier account for 90 days or more. You also must process at least $20,000 in annual PayPal sales (Premier account), or $15,000 in annual PayPal sales (Business account). You also need to pay off any existing PayPal Working Capital loans before applying.

CHAPTER 4

Tapping Friends and Family

Next to credit cards and personal savings, loans from friends and family are the most popular way entrepreneurs fund their ventures. There are both pros and cons to this. On one hand, raising money from your personal network can also be a step toward securing money from future investors, because it demonstrates you are grounded in a network of family and acquaintances who have already bought into the business plan. On the other, you risk losing friends and straining relationships with relatives. Your next holiday party won't be as fun if half the people there think you fleeced them or are annoyed because you went on vacation before paying them back.

This chapter talks about how to borrow money from friends, relatives, community members, and professional contacts (even ex-bosses!)—without jeopardizing your relationships or their livelihood.

You may be skirting the bank by getting a loan from family or friends, but you should still treat the situation as strictly business. Putting the agreement in writing not only protects both parties, but also your relationship. After all, borrowing money is not the same as borrowing the car.

Basics of Borrowing from Friends and Family

Borrowing from friends and family makes sense. People with whom you have close relationships know you are reliable and competent, so there should be no problem in asking for a loan, right? Well . . . while borrowing money from family and friends may seem an easy alternative to dealing with bankers, it can actually be a much more delicate situation and it's important to be as disciplined as you would be in dealing with a professional investor.

Here are some basic rules:

> *Treat them as if they were strangers.* Forget for the moment that your investor is a friend or relative. Make it an "arm's length" transaction, and insist on the same sort of legal documentation you would prepare if they were a total stranger. Why? Because too many entrepreneurs borrow money from family and friends on an informal basis. The terms of the loan have been verbalized, but not written down in a contract.

> *Check with a lawyer.* Lending money can be tricky for people who can't view the transaction at arm's length; if they don't feel you're running your business correctly, they might try to interfere. In some cases, you can't prevent this even with a written contract, because many states guarantee voting rights to an individual who has invested money in a business. This can create a lot of hard feelings. Make sure to check with your attorney before accepting any loans from friends or family. So, if it's a loan, have your lawyer prepare an IOU (called a "promissory note") for the friend or relative, and don't offer less than a commercial interest rate.

≫ *Tie all payments to your cash flow.* Try to avoid obligations with fixed repayment schedules. Consider instead "cash flow" obligations, in which your investor will receive a percentage of your operating cash flow (if any) until they have either been repaid in full with interest, or have achieved a specified percentage return on their investment.

Types of Transactions

When borrowing from friends or family, the loan—or transaction—can be treated as a gift, a loan, or an equity investment in the business. Each has pluses and minuses, which are outlined here.

Gifts

The best thing about a gift is that you don't have to pay it back. But you probably won't raise as much as you would if you were offering a potential return on the money. Also, gifts can quickly turn into loans in the minds of friends and relatives should you succeed. A signed document—even a letter saying the money was given—will protect you down the road.

Loans

Many experts suggest loans as the optimal way for friends and family to invest because there are set repayment terms. They will know how long it will take for them to get their money back and at what interest rate. (If you are current with repayments, you can also avoid drawing their ire should you spend money on yourself.) A business attorney can easily draw up a promissory note detailing the terms of the loan. An SBA blog entry suggests another strategy to formalize the relationship: structuring the loan through a peer-to-peer (P2P) lending company that will act as an intermediary, collecting the payments from you for a fee. Of course, one downside of borrowing is that you are tying up some of your business's cash flow in the repayments.

Equity

If the transaction is treated as equity, you don't have to pay the loaner back until you make a profit or cash out, but you are literally turning a friend or a relative into a business partner if you give them an ownership stake in the company. If one or a few of your friends and relatives have business savvy, great. Bringing them on as investors transforms them into motivated advisors. Plus, they will likely be more forgiving than outside investors when it comes to your business's ups and downs.

However, you will want a business lawyer involved in this. Consider whether you want this person as a business partner. He or she will have a right to tell you how to run the venture. This can be highly beneficial if your acquaintance/investor has entrepreneurial experience or other useful know-how, but it can quickly become an annoyance otherwise. You also risk straining the relationship should you move on to another venture.

Worth considering are convertible notes, which are an investment option popular for startup businesses. When an investor buys a convertible note, they are in essence giving a loan with the option of being paid back with equity in the company down the road. Convertible notes typically have a maturity date, at which point the loan must be repaid to the investor with interest.

However you proceed, it is always advisable to present a formal business plan when pitching to prospective investors—even friends and relatives. But you don't need to present printed materials and charts up front. Rather, it is best to lay out your business plans verbally, because those in your personal network will likely base their decision on trust. The "kitchen table pitch" is really about selling yourself. Be frank about the risks, and explain what the money will go toward and how it will grow the business. Then follow up with written materials later.

Finally, be prepared for some tough love. Especially if it is a friend or relative who knows something about starting or running a business, their point of view may be just what you need.

But remember that, in some cases, debt may actually be better than equity. If someone lends you money, you only have to pay it back, with interest. They can't tell you how to run your company. If someone buys stock in your business, they are legally your business partner. When in doubt, make it a loan, and pay it back as soon as you can.

Winding Up for the Pitch: The Right Way to Ask Your Parents to Finance Your Business

Alex Genadinik borrowed $20,000 from his mom to launch Problemio, a startup that makes mobile apps for small businesses. Since 2012, Carlo Cisco has taken $150,000 in convertible-note investments from his relatives to expand Select, his New York City dining, travel, and entertainment discount club. And Andrew Angus has borrowed $500,000 from his mom (half her net worth) to keep up with the exponential growth of Switch Video, his animated video production company, which was acquired by Vidyard in 2015.

None of these transactions came without consequence or regret. "It might be the easiest money to get," Cisco says, "but it's probably going to be the most important money that you ever have, because you're not going to want to let them down."

If you plan to spend your holidays with your family hitting up Mom and Dad for startup cash, first listen carefully to what these entrepreneurs recommend:

▷ *Invest your own money first.* (See Chapter 2 for more on bootstrapping.) Cisco, a former Groupon staffer, burned through $40,000 of his savings to launch FoodFan, a restaurant-review website that was the precursor to Select. A $100,000 convertible note from investors helped him forge relationships with restaurants and create an early version of his platform. By the time he asked his family for cash, FoodFan listed 850,000 restaurants and 50,000 menus. "We had an incredible brand name and a massive amount of data," Cisco says.

▷ *Solicit strangers.* Third-party validation from outside financiers can strengthen your pitch to the parents. Angus, who launched his business in 2006 in Collingwood, Ontario, says a $250,000 loan from Canada's Centre for Business and Economic Development helped him sell his mother on his plans. Angus' mom opened a home equity line of credit to pay off his loan at a lower rate, and she now has a convertible-note investment in the company, to be paid back in five years with a 6 percent annual interest rate.

Cisco seconds the suggestion to tap outside investors. He turned to relatives only after several angel investors offered him amounts ranging from $25,000 to $100,000 each in exchange for 6 to 10 percent equity—slices of the pie he felt were too big to give away. Through convertible-note loans from his family, Cisco held off on negotiating a price for his company too early. When he finally did raise an additional $150,000 from outside investors, his family's stake in the company converted to straight equity.

❯ *Get it in writing.* Genadinik admits he regrets the "very, very informal" loan agreement he made with his mother. There was no timetable, no interest rate, no contract, nothing. Roughly six months later, his mom wanted her $20,000 back. Although Problemio had revenue by then, Genadinik didn't have the cash lying around. Rather than ruffle Mom's feathers, he took out a short-term microloan and sold $15,000 in stock to pay her back, incurring unwanted interest and costs in the process. Lesson learned: Sign a contract with family financiers so that expectations are crystal clear.

❯ *Don't ask for too much.* If Switch Video had failed, Angus' mom would have lost her home. Fortunately, business took off, with more than $2 million in annual revenue and customers such as Facebook, IBM, HP, Microsoft, and American Express, culminating in a move to the San Francisco Bay Area and, later, the acquisition by Vidyard.

Select founder Cisco cautions against borrowing more than your parents can afford to lose. "You do want the amount to be enough that you have a shot," he says. "But you don't want it to be so much that someone has a problem if it doesn't work out." Remember, you will have to face these people for many holiday gatherings to come.

Family Money in a Nutshell: Pros and Cons

Simply put, there are advantages and disadvantages to using family money. These are the pros and cons, boiled down.

Pros

- Highly likely to say yes
- Better financing and equity terms
- Faster access to cash

Cons

- Relatives meddling in the business
- Smirks from industry insiders
- Lifetime of guilt if startup tanks

What to Watch Out For: Some Hard Truths

Have you heard of FFF money? FFF stands for family, friends, and fools. Many new entrepreneurs receive the initial funding for their businesses from people close to them, causing these relationships to start sliding toward disaster. Over his 15-year career as an entrepreneur, Josh Steimle borrowed from all three groups. This section offers his perspective on what to watch out for when borrowing FFF money.

Although some of these funding arrangements have happy endings, all too many end painfully, with consequences ranging from unfortunate to disastrous. Before considering FFF money as an easy way to start your business, consider the following.

Money Changes People

Nobody starts out in a marriage saying, "How can I use money to ruin this relationship?" But many couples seemingly do. Financial disagreements are the number-one predictor of divorce in the United States, according to one study. The person you dated and were madly in love with before you married can become another person entirely when finances enter the picture.

Money changes people in business relationships as well. Finances will cause contention when there isn't enough, when there's too much, and at every point in between, no matter how great a person you are or the lender is.

The Borrower Is Enslaved to the Lender

Many have said that the day you take a loan from someone, you are beholden until you pay off the last cent. The lender may claim that they don't mind and just want to help you succeed.

But wait until you take a vacation in Hawaii, buy a new house or car, or even choose a more expensive dish at a restaurant than he or she does. Then the lender might start thinking, "Wait a second. I gave this guy a loan and he's spending money on this instead of paying me back?"

Your Business May Fail

Most small businesses do. Think yours will be the exception? So did the roughly half of U.S. business owners who shut down their companies within the first five years of doing business.

What's your plan if your great idea doesn't work out? Will you feel OK telling investors you're sorry you lost their money, or will you feel obligated to turn investments into loans and pay them back? In the latter case, what will be your plan for paying the loans off?

Tips on Avoiding Trouble—From Firsthand Experience

Here's some advice Steimle gave his dad that he feels can be broadly applied to anyone considering borrowing from a family member or friend—some of which echoes the warnings given earlier in this chapter:

> ▷ *The dynamic should resemble that at a bank, not one between relatives.* Repayment should be required. Payment terms can be flexible, but the borrower should not be let out of the loan. This is for the borrower's sake, not the lender's, because the lesson learned otherwise is that it's OK to borrow money from people and not pay it back. That's not a good lesson for anyone of any age to learn.
> ▷ *Set up a payment schedule.* If the new business isn't generating enough income to repay the loan, the borrower should earn the money some other way and send the payment every month, no matter what. A penalty should be charged for late payment any month a payment is missed and every month thereafter until the borrower catches up.

▷ *Pay interest.* The way the real world works is by charging interest on loans. If the borrower wants to pay less interest, repayment should take place faster.

The Legal Agreement: Keeping Things Strictly Business

Going into debt to start a business is less than ideal in almost all circumstances. Borrowing from family and friends risks incurring personal fallout. But when this is the only way to start or fund a business, following these steps can greatly reduce that risk.

First, you must state how much money you need, what you'll use it for, and how you'll pay it back. Next, draw up the legal papers—an agreement stating that the person will indeed put money into the business.

Most important, says Mike McKeever, author of *How to Write a Business Plan*: "Outline the legal responsibilities of both parties and when and how the money should be paid back." If your loan agreement is complex, it's a good idea to consult your accountant about the best ways to structure the loan.

Too frequently, business owners fail to take the time to figure out exactly what kind of paperwork they should complete when they borrow from family or friends. "Often small business owners put more thought into figuring out what type of car to buy than how to structure this type of lending arrangement," says Steven I. Levey, now-retired senior principal and CEO of accounting firm GHP Horwath. Unfortunately, once you've made an error in this area, it's difficult to correct it.

Your loan agreement needs to specify whether the loan is secured (that is, the lender holds title to part of your property) or unsecured, what the payments will be, when they're due, and what the interest is. If the money is in the form of an investment, you have to establish whether the business is a partnership or corporation and what role, if any, the investor will play.

Whichever route you take, make sure the agreement is in writing.

Dealing with the IRS: Tax Considerations

Putting the agreement on paper also protects both you and your lender come tax time. Relying on informal and verbal agreements results in tax quagmires. "In these cases, you have a burden of proof to show the IRS that [the money] was not a gift," says Tom Ochsenschlager, former vice president of taxation for the American Institute of Certified Public Accountants. If the IRS views it as a gift because there was no intention to repay it, then the lender becomes subject to the federal gift tax rules and will have to pay taxes on any amount in excess of $14,000.

Also make sure the person providing the money charges an interest rate that reflects a fair market value. If your friend or family member wants to give you a no-interest loan, make sure the loan is less than $100,000. If you borrow more, the IRS will slap on what it considers to be market-rate interest, better known as "imputed interest," on the lender. That means that while your friend or relative may not be receiving any interest on the money you borrowed, the IRS will tax them as if they were.

No interest is imputed if the aggregate loans are less than $10,000. Between $10,000 and $100,000, the imputed amount is limited to your net investment income, such as interest, dividends, and in some cases capital gains. To determine the interest rate on these transactions, the IRS uses what it calls the Applicable Federal Rate (AFR), which changes monthly. Keep in mind that if you don't put all the details of the loan in writing, it will be very difficult for you to deduct the interest you pay on it. Additionally, the relative who lent the money won't be able to take a tax deduction on the loss if you find you can't repay.

To be absolutely safe, Ochsenschlager recommends that you make the friend or relative who is providing the money one of the business' shareholders. This effectively makes the transaction an investment in your company and also makes it easier from a tax standpoint for your friend or relative to write off the transaction as an ordinary loss if the business fails. (This applies only if the total amount your company received for its stock, including the relative's investment, does not exceed $1 million.)

In addition, "If your company is wildly successful, your relative will have an equity interest in the business, and his or her original investment will be worth quite a bit more," Ochsenschlager says. In contrast, if a relative gives you a loan and your company goes under, the relative's loss would generally be considered a personal bad debt. This creates more of a tax disadvantage because personal bad debts can be claimed as capital losses only to offset capital gains. If the capital loss exceeds the capital gains, only $3,000 of the loss can be used against ordinary income in any given year. Thus, an individual making a large loan that isn't repaid may have to wait several years to realize the tax benefits from the loss.

If the loan that can't be repaid is a business loan, however, the lender receives a deduction against ordinary income and can take deductions even before the loan becomes totally worthless. (One catch: The IRS takes a very narrow view of what qualifies as a business loan. To qualify, the loan would have to be connected to the lender's business.) Consult an accountant about the best way to structure the loan for maximum tax benefits to both parties.

Making your relative a shareholder doesn't mean you'll have to put up with Mom or Pop meddling in the business. Depending on your company's organizational structure, your friend or relative can be a silent partner—an investor whose involvement in the business is limited to providing capital, rather than making operational or other decisions about running the business—if it is set up as a partnership or a silent shareholder if you are organized as an S corporation or limited liability company.

Even with every detail documented, your responsibilities are far from over. Don't make assumptions or take people for granted just because they are friends or family members. Communication is key. If your relative or friend is not actively involved in the business, make sure you contact him or her every month or two to explain how the business is going. "When people invest in small businesses, it often becomes sort of their pet project," says McKeever. "It's important to take the time to keep them informed."

And, of course, there are the payments. Though friends or relatives who invest in your business understand the risks, you must never take the loan for granted. "Don't be cavalier about paying the money back," McKeever says. "That kind of attitude could ruin the relationship."

Turn Your Customers into Investors

Zak Cassady-Dorion wanted to aggressively expand Pure Mountain Olive Oil, his gourmet olive oil business. When the bank denied the loan and he needed to open a second shop, he found a better backer: loyal customer Wolfgang Foust.

Foust, who grew up in Spain with olive trees in the backyard, routinely traveled 70 miles to shop at Pure Mountain's inaugural Rhinebeck, New York, store, which opened in May 2012. Foust invested $10,000 in Pure Mountain in exchange for a small piece of equity. That August, Cassady-Dorion opened his second shop in Tarrytown, just miles from Foust's home.

"It was a real testament to what we were doing that he wanted us to open up a shop closer to him," Cassady-Dorion says.

Foust, a former produce trader, joined the company as COO and general manager when the Tarrytown store opened, and remained in the role for more than three years.

Enthusiastic customers and community members make great investors, says Mike Moyer, a serial entrepreneur who teaches entrepreneurship at Northwestern University and the University of Chicago Booth School of Business. "They're the ones who'll spread the word about your business," he says.

Of course, there's more to scoring capital from community cheerleaders than mentioning you're looking to expand and sussing out whether they have money to burn. Here's what you need to know:

> ▷ *Accept investments, not loans.* Moyer cautions against personal loans when accepting money from a neighbor or customer: "For small money—under $50,000—I always point people toward a convertible loan or convertible equity note." That way, he explains, if the company goes under, there's no expectation of repayment.

> ▷ *Get it in writing.* Don't rely on a handshake—there's too much room for disagreement later. Don't fly blind when creating a contract, either. "If you don't have a really good understanding of what equity is and how it works, have somebody else who is more experienced take a look," says Cassady-Dorion, who tapped his financial advisor for contract help.

> ▷ *Set the level of involvement.* Most people who make a modest investment in your company won't become a senior executive like Pure Mountain's Foust. To discourage investors from acting like one, set boundaries early. "It's important they know that you have the control," Cassady-Dorion says. "If they have 2, 3, 4, 5, or 10 percent

equity in your company, you don't want them calling you up and telling you how to run your business every other day."

How Much Is It Worth?

Some quick tips on pricing your equity stakes:

- Give yourself a pre-revenue valuation of $1 million. For new companies in nearly any business, this is a safe place to start: not so high that you scare off investors, and not so low that you sell yourself short.
- Receiving a $50,000 investment bumps up your valuation to $1,050,000; therefore, the equity on that investment ($50,000/$1,050,000) = 4.76 percent.
- If stumped, seek advice from business mentors, advisors, and peers who've been there.
- For contract help, get referrals for a startup lawyer near you who offers "startup rates" and has structured startup equity deals before.

TrustLeaf: Making Raising Money Easier for All Involved

Joe Meisch had already invested tens of thousands of dollars in the temple massager he developed to relieve tension headaches. But he needed a few thousand more to finish updating the product based on feedback from beta users.

He'd already tapped friends and family while building his original prototype several years back, so he figured that well had run dry. This time Meisch turned to TrustLeaf, a platform that formalizes friends-and-family fundraising by offering free personal loan agreements using attorney-prepared templates.

The Meisch clan was impressed. Joe's sister, brother-in-law, and a family friend invested $2,500 in all. Now the former U.S. Army reservist, who had formerly donated his massagers to combat veterans, is finally selling them online to the public.

Since TrustLeaf launched in 2014, dozens of companies have raised several hundred thousand dollars in fundraising campaigns on the platform, says CEO Anson Liang. Add in borrowers who have used TrustLeaf's contract templates without creating a campaign on the site, and that number jumps to $41 million, he says, with loans averaging $48,000 at up to 10 percent interest.

Liang, a Founder Institute alumnus and serial entrepreneur who knows firsthand the awkwardness of asking loved ones for a loan, built TrustLeaf along with head of business development Daniel Lieser. Their goal: to help the 38 percent of small business owners who tap friends and relatives for starter capital each year. "It just takes the stress and emotion out of the combination of family and money," Liang says.

Fundraising campaigns posted on TrustLeaf are not public; they're visible only to people the campaign creator invites by email. "That's actually one of the key differentiators of our site," Liang says. "A lot of people want to keep their business idea and their fundraising process private, especially when asking friends and family for money."

There's no minimum ask for fundraising campaigns on the site, which tend to span 30 to 45 days. Borrowers can invite as many supporters to contribute to their campaigns as they want. They can also suggest several potential loan amounts and repayment scenarios.

Attorney Curtis Mo, a partner at global law firm DLA Piper and a TrustLeaf board member, created the site's template loan agreement. Entrepreneurs plug in the names, loan amount, terms, and interest rate, and then both lender and borrower sign the document online, where it's accessible 24/7. No private financial data is required to create a campaign or contract on the site.

Borrowers can use TrustLeaf's tracking and communication tools to keep tabs on payments and update lenders on their business's progress. The ability to accept loans and repay borrowers through the site is coming, Liang says; the same goes for a convertible equity note template founders can use for loved ones who would rather be repaid in company shares than interest.

The formal contract and ease of use made believers out of Meisch and his family. "They made the process organized and added a sense of legitimacy to what I was doing instead of me just picking up the phone and asking, 'Hey, can you loan me another $1,000?'" he says.

Armed with the additional funds, Meisch was able to stay in business long enough to attract the attention of Walter Reed National Military Medical Center, which has conducted trials with his product on PTSD patients.

Able: This Company Will Give You a Loan—But There's a Catch

When the opportunity to buy an established hair salon fell into Hayley Groll's lap, she quickly took stock of her financing options. The veteran hairstylist was not approved by the online lender she initially contacted. Then she found Austin-based Able, which bills itself as a "collaborative lender."

Within three weeks, Groll had a three-year, $105,000 loan, enough to buy Shag Salon and renew its 1,850-square-foot commercial lease for a decade. Even better was her interest rate: 9 percent.

The brainchild of Harvard MBAs Will Davis and Evan Baehr, Able offers business owners one- to three-year loans of $25,000 to $250,000 at 8 to 16 percent interest—but with a twist: Borrowers must raise the first 25 percent from friends and family.

"What we're really doing is trying to find the people who are being missed by traditional banks and even nontraditional online lenders," Davis says.

Able conducted a beta test prior to its official launch in 2014, tweaking the terms and procedures with each loan. That year, the online lender made 50 loans ranging from $5,000 to $150,000, mostly in the Austin area, but received nearly $40 million in loan requests from entrepreneurs nationwide.

How It Works

To qualify for a loan, businesses must be at least six months old. Davis wouldn't stipulate revenue requirements but says Able's borrowers to date make $1 million or less annually.

After a business owner fills out an online application, Able uses its proprietary technology to assess the company's bank accounts, cash flow, and credit history—pretty standard stuff. What's new is that Able's algorithm also looks at a company's social media following and reviews via Yelp, Facebook, Twitter, and LinkedIn. Davis wouldn't reveal how a business's online footprint is weighted or what metrics help or hinder an applicant, but he claims Able gains a more complete picture of a company's creditworthiness than any bank can acquire.

Finding Backers

Once Able gives the green light, borrowers need to line up at least three backers (friends, relatives, mentors, colleagues, or customers) to collectively kick in 25 percent of the approved loan. Backers must contribute at least $1,000 each, and family cannot contribute more than half of the 25 percent. Hairstylist Groll received $30,000 in all from five backers, including three long-standing clients. (Able's software automatically confirms that backers and borrowers are indeed acquainted.)

Depending on how fast the borrower lines up backers, funding can arrive within two weeks of applying, "much quicker than traditional bank financing," Davis says.

What It Costs

In addition to APR rates, Able charges a loan origination fee of 3 percent, but there are no early-repayment or other fees. Borrowers choose whether they want to repay the loan in one, two, or three years, and Able's platform handles repaying the backers directly.

Although Able dictates the APR of its 75 percent loan contribution, the individual backers providing the other 25 percent are free to choose their own interest rates. Able takes their terms and blends everyone's interest rates into one composite rate.

"In some cases," Davis says, "some of the backers come in with a lower APR rate that reduces the overall interest rate of the loan itself."

CHAPTER 5

Winning Grants, Contests, and Pitch Slams

While no one can guarantee you'll win a contest, it's definitely worth a shot. You certainly can't win if you don't enter.

These days, dozens of business schools and universities host business plan contests, some with cash prizes as high as $100,000. Multiple states, including Wisconsin, Virginia, and New York, sponsor contests, too. But money isn't the only reason to enter a business plan competition. You'll also get a chance to run your plan past an audience of venture capitalists and angel investors, who may decide to fund it whether you win or not.

Universities, governments, and corporations offer grants and hold thousands of small business plan contests and pitch slams each year. A grant is a non-repayable monetary award given to support a specific business or project. These are often made available through universities, private foundations, government agencies, or nongovernmental organizations. A pitch slam is a type of competition that involves delivering a succinct pitch for your business—usually just a few minutes—to a panel of judges or investors in the hopes of convincing them to invest. It's like speed-dating, for business funding.

How do you find these funding opportunities, and how can you determine which are right for you? What should you look for—and look out for?

Let's start with taking a look at something everybody dreams of: free money.

Seeking Grants from the Government

"But wait," you may be thinking. "I'm not a nonprofit—I can't get a grant." Well, it turns out, nonprofits aren't the only organizations eligible for government grants. For example, from 2010–2014, for-profit company Canopy Apps received $2 million in National Institutes of Health (NIH) grants to develop translation technology for medical professionals working with patients who don't speak English.

Jerrit Tan, former CEO of New York City–based Canopy, believes more entrepreneurs should take advantage of the billions of dollars in business grants offered by government agencies, which can buy a startup valuable R&D time and boost credibility.

"You're literally turning stacks of paper [grant applications] into money for your business," Tan says. "And the government usually does not take equity."

The qualifications for winning a government grant vary depending on the grant program to which you are applying. In general, though, eligibility for a grant requires that the business be registered—as a corporation, LLC, partnership, or sole proprietorship—and that it fit into a specific sector— such as health care, technology, or energy. Most government grants are awarded to purposeful businesses, such as those focused on development, research, job creation, or new technologies or products.

Of course, nabbing local, state, and federal grants involves more than cutting and pasting your business plan into an application. This section discusses what you should consider.

Understanding Grants

Business owners often turn to grants because they are not required to pay them back; essentially, you can look at grants as "free money," although they come with stipulations. Also, understanding and navigating the grant process can be complex.

First you have to research and find a grant for which you're eligible. Then you have to understand the strict application and compliance guidelines you must meet to be eligible. You must devote time and energy to the lengthy application process, and then wait for approval. You have to compete with other businesses for the same pool of money. And finally, if you're awarded a grant, you must report on how you used it. In a nutshell, you need to have all your ducks in a row, up front and afterward.

Aim High

A revolutionary idea is essential, says Tan, whose translation app targets the language barriers that plague 15 percent of U.S. patients. "Incremental ideas usually don't win," he says. "It's almost like the crazier, the better—within reason. This is the government, after all."

It's essential to be able to quantify the effect your product will have on the market, says Amy Baxter, an Atlanta pediatric emergency doctor who in 2009 scored $1.1 million in NIH funding for Buzzy, a pain-blocking device used for administering injections to children. "Make it clear how big the impact of the problem you want to solve is," she says, "and how inadequate the previous solutions are. Even better is to have a way to measure how well your solution is working."

Put in the Time

For large federal grants, expect to spend several months preparing an application.

"It's not a fast process," says Michael Patterson, COO at SimUCare USA and former CEO of Graphene Frontiers in Philadelphia, an advanced materials and nanotechnology company that has won 10 grants from local, state, and federal agencies totaling nearly $1.3 million. Payments can be slow to arrive, too. To tide you over, he says, "You have to have funding from other sources or be able to get other funding quickly, whether that's revenue or equity investments or something else."

Find the Right Opportunities

"There are grants out there that can be more trouble than they're worth," Patterson warns. Some have big payouts but overly restrictive stipulations on how the money can be used. Others seem almost too good to be true, and in most cases it probably is.

But don't discount smaller grants. Many have less stringent application requirements and spending restrictions. A $2,000 grant Graphene received from a Pennsylvania economic development program was designed to support larger grant-writing opportunities. Graphene used the money to bankroll proposal efforts for a hefty Department of Defense grant.

Get External Feedback

When pursuing a grant, Canopy runs its application by "as many smart people as we can find," Tan says. The more removed from the business reviewers are, the more likely it is they'll find the hidden flaws in the proposal.

Outsiders may also come up with new commercialization ideas. In Canopy's case, that meant selling the translation app to the legal, construction, travel, and education sectors, industries the NIH has no vested interest in. As Tan points out, even with a grant, "it's still up to you to find other ways to commercialize your product."

Finding Grants for Women-Owned Businesses

Many business owners think federal grants are just a click away. We have all seen the ads promoting free federal money to start a business, but this is a huge misconception. While there are federal grants available in the areas of medical research, science, education, and technology development, no such grants exist specifically for women-owned businesses. You may find grants funding projects that empower women, but such funding is often set aside for nonprofit corporations, not for-profit businesses.

When researching grants specifically for a woman-owned business, start at the state level. Most states offer grants for women-owned businesses in some capacity. Each state website has a business section where you can find grant and funding opportunities for women. A good example of this is the business section for the state of New York, which lists incentives and programs for businesses. Check out your state's site to find out what is available for your business.

Private Grants for Women

To help in your search, here's some information on a few private grants for women:

⟩ *The Eileen Fisher Women-Owned Business Grant Program* (www.eileenfisher.com/grants/women-owned-business/women-owned-business-overview). Five grants are awarded annually. The businesses must be 100 percent women-owned and have founding principles of social consciousness, sustainability, and innovation, plus be ready to move to the next phase of development.

⟩ *FedEx Opportunity Knocks Small Business Grant Contest* (http://smallbusinessgrant.fedex.com). Applicants are encouraged to share their visions to receive a portion of the $100,000 awarded in grants. Part of the judging involves the general public voting for the finalists, so participants may also promote their businesses while garnering votes.

⟩ *Idea Café Small Business Grant* (www.businessownersideacafe.com/small_business_grants/). The Idea Café is a free gateway that hosts different grants on its site. One grant is the Small Business Grant, which awards a $1,000 grand prize to a single business with the most innovative idea. Visitors to the site vote for the winner.

▷ *InnovateHER: Innovating for Women Business Challenge* (www.sba. gov/offices/headquarters/wbo/resources/1465581). This business challenge is sponsored by the SBA's Office of Women's Business Ownership. The top three finalists split $70,000 in prize money for submitting ideas that have an impact on the lives of women.

▷ *Small Business Innovation Research* (www.epa.gov/sbir). Eleven different federal agencies participate in this awards-based program, which incentivizes and enables small businesses to explore their technological potential.

▷ *Small Business Technology Transfer Program* (www.sbir.gov/about/about-sttr). The STTR program reserves a specific percentage of federal research and development funding to provide funding opportunities to small businesses.

▷ *Zions Bank—Smart Women Grants* (www.zionsbank.com/learning-center/swsm-grant.jsp). This Utah-based bank's grant annually awards $3,000 across six different categories, including business.

Private Grants for Minority-Owned Businesses

Another great resource is the Minority Business Development Agency (MBDA), online at www.mbda.gov. The MBDA is an agency of the U.S. Department of Commerce that assists minorities in establishing and growing their businesses. On its site, you can research grants and access links to state agencies that work with women-owned businesses for funding opportunities. The MBDA provides a list of state agencies at www.mbda.gov/node/1429.

Applying for a Grant

Once you find a funding opportunity, there are multiple steps required to apply. Here are a few tips to assist you:

▷ Make sure your business is eligible for the grant: Read the grant synopsis guidelines and eligibility requirements.

- Create a checklist for all the required documents.
- Follow the rules. Grant applications can be very technical. It wouldn't hurt to have a second (or even third) set of eyes review the application to ensure you have provided all necessary documents.
- Start early. Since the application process can sometimes be long, it doesn't hurt to get a jump on things.

If you find the grant application process too daunting or lengthy, online lender Kabbage (www.kabbage.com) is committed to supporting small business loans for women business owners (see Chapter 8 for more on alternative lending). Because its application process is fully automated and online, Kabbage can quickly provide small business loans of up to $100,000. It uses simple, meaningful revenue data from your business to approve your loan—not elaborate documentation that takes extensive time to gather.

Hometown Glory: Get Startup Grants and Seed Investments from Your City

After earning an MBA from the Wharton School of the University of Pennsylvania, Ashrit Kamireddi was prepared to go wherever he had to in order to raise seed money to grow VeryApt, his apartment review platform. But thanks to a $100,000 angel investment from Philadelphia's StartUp PHL program, which invests in local entrepreneurs, he didn't have to leave town. Kamireddi has since hired four full-time employees, raised a total of $270,000 in seed funds, and expanded his operations to 11 other cities. Philly, which launched its $6 million startup fund in 2012, is among several major cities offering grants and seed investments for entrepreneurs. Among them, Detroit boasts two venture funds for early-stage companies, with a portfolio of nearly 80 startups; Denver awards $35,000 in annual grants to new companies.

So what's the best way to gain access to these funds? To identify opportunities, check with your city's economic development office, incubators, accelerators, coworking spaces, networking groups, and anywhere else startup founders and advisors congregate. Begin building relationships long before you're ready to raise capital—even a year or two in advance, advises Archna Sahay, Philadelphia's director of entrepreneurial investment, who regularly counsels entrepreneurs about pitching StartUp PHL. "The minute you realize you want to take on the investment is when you need to start having that conversation," she says.

City information sessions on startup grants and seed funds are a great place to start. Be sure to introduce yourself to key players while there. Also set up one-on-ones with stakeholders receptive to meeting with you.

"Don't be shy about asking to run things by them," says Bethlehem, Pennsylvania–based Steve Boerner, founder and managing director of Hatch House, a 12-month live-work program for entrepreneurs in or just out of college. Boerner turned to Asher Schiavone—economic development coordinator for the city of Bethlehem, which has awarded millions in business grants to local startups since 2004—who offered suggestions on everything from what to include in the application to the details of his slide deck to his pitch. That dialogue led to Boerner landing $15,000 from the city.

Prepare thoroughly for these meetups so you can speak with authority about your venture. Make that chance count by understanding the fund's motives. Municipal governments have good reasons for giving money to startups—mainly job creation and economic stimulation. Be sure your goals align with those of the investment program and that you are clear on all stipulations, advises Kamireddi, whose equity investment from Philadelphia came with the caveat that VeryApt stay local for a minimum of 18 months.

To gain extra intel, Kamireddi suggests talking to entrepreneurs in the city's investment portfolio about their experiences with the program.

"Often people think it's just about the dollars," says Patricia Glaza, vice president and managing director at Invest Detroit, which runs the city's community development funds. But ensuring that an investor's agenda meshes with yours is equally important. Also key: the mentorship that comes with the funding. For Jonathan Frankel, founder of Nucleus, a wireless intercom that scored $100,000 from StartUp PHL in 2015, having the ear of Josh Kopelman, partner at First Round Capital, the VC firm that manages and selects StartUp PHL's investments, sweetened the deal. "You want to take smart money," Frankel says. "You want to take money that comes with good advice."

Entering Contests: Bringing Your "A" Game

While grants are awarded by government entities for a specific purpose, such as research and development, contests are often sponsored by venture capitalists, angel investors, or corporations and universities and are geared toward startups and early-stage businesses. Contests usually involve delivering a pitch or presentation and, unlike grants that are not required to be repaid, competition winnings are usually structured as an investment on the part of the party awarding the funding.

Prizes from business contests run the gamut. A seemingly infinite number of local and business school competitions offer small-change awards of $5,000 to $15,000; meanwhile, Rice University doles out six-figure prizes annually, as do accelerators MassChallenge and Techstars.

For Jen Barnett, winning two business plan competitions was about more than just prize money and bragging rights—it made it possible to launch her company.

In July 2011, the Birmingham, Alabama–based web and marketing strategist and her partner, web designer Sam Brasseale, won the incubate!(bang) business contest with their idea for a marketplace for fresh, local food. In addition to $30,000 in seed money, the Alabama contest awarded them $50,000 worth of web programming services, three months of free office space, and mentorship on everything from honing their business model to incorporating. "Those were exactly the gaps we needed filled," Barnett says. "It has completely transformed our lives."

Although it is now closed, Freshfully.com launched in November 2011 to immediate success, exponentially surpassing Barnett and Brasseale's projections. The pioneering online shop sold locally grown food. But the duo didn't stop there. In March 2012, they won another local business plan competition (run by a brewery and a neighborhood revitalization group). Besides a slew of publicity, the two received expert guidance from seasoned Birmingham business owners, plus six months of free office and retail space.

"We have not made any financial contributions ourselves," Barnett says. "We don't make huge salaries. But we also didn't have any money to start the business, and we did not have to take on any debt." Bennet and Brasseale have since moved on to other ventures. Barnett opened a wine and beer shop and is now a digital strategist and marketing consultant; Brasseale is director of interactive at another Alabama company, Cayenne Creative.

Work Your Niche

So which competitions should you enter? How will you dazzle the judges? And how can you walk away a winner even if you don't place? Don't just throw everything against the wall and see what sticks. Be selective about the contests you enter; choose those that focus on your market and/or business sector. This doesn't just winnow the competition; it also gets you in front of judges who know the community or industry you're hoping to take by storm.

For Jennifer Medbery, founder and CEO of Kickboard, an online student-data tracking program for educators, this meant focusing on contests for educational startups and businesses in New Orleans, where she's based. Between 2009 and 2012, she raised more than $150,000 in seed money from five wins.

But this strategy isn't just about money. Staying within your niche will get you targeted feedback from veteran investors and business leaders in your specific field. "Pitching to people in the industry is going to help you hone the pitch that much faster," Medbery says. "You're then much better prepared when you talk to venture capital and angel investors."

Medbery capitalized on both: She won $25,000 in 2010 from the Milken-Penn GSE Business Plan Competition, offered by the University of Pennsylvania, and nabbed two of the contest's judges as close business advisors. "That kind of access to senior leaders has been invaluable," she says. "Because these aren't the kind of people where you could just send them an email."

Think beyond the Money

Contests aren't just for newbies seeking seed funding, professional services, and free advice. Young companies that have nailed down their business models and begun reaching out to customers, partners, and investors can benefit, too.

Tim Faley, former managing director of the Zell Lurie Institute at the University of Michigan's Ross School of Business and current Sokoloff Professor of Entrepreneurship at the University of the Virgin Islands in

St. Thomas, agrees. "All the students tell us that the money's nice, but the feedback's invaluable," says Faley. In fact, he advises founders of early-stage startups to pursue contests that emphasize feedback and mentorship over financial awards. "If you're more developed, then you go into the competition to build awareness," Faley says.

Jake Irvin knows firsthand how becoming a finalist in a high-profile competition can put a recently launched company on the map. After winning first place in the 2012 U.S. Imagine Cup, a student technology competition sponsored by Microsoft, Irvin received a flurry of media attention for his Tempe, Arizona, company, FlashFood, which delivers restaurant and catering leftovers to food banks and shelters.

"This has been great for us in reaching out to the public," says Irvin, who founded the business with six Arizona State University classmates. Several charities, food recovery groups, and national grocery and restaurant chains have since contacted FlashFood to partner with the company.

Some contest wins come not with a check but with something equally valuable. In March 2012, Medbery's Kickboard won the New Orleans Entrepreneur Week Coulter Challenge. The grand prize: a trip to San Francisco to pitch investors. "It was exactly the right prize for Kickboard at the time," Medbery says, noting it's "near impossible" to place a price tag on the insights she gleaned from the financiers and business analysts she met—not to mention the relationships she forged with potential investors, advisors, and senior leaders at the region's public schools.

Of course, you have to be in a position to take advantage of such opportunities if they come your way. "Simply being introduced to a venture capitalist doesn't make a six-figure angel investment appear," Medbery says. "It's up to you as the entrepreneur to build authentic relationships with potential investors and advisors."

Do Your Homework

Winning a competition requires far more than a well-researched, passionately conveyed idea. One way to up your game is to seek feedback from entrepreneurs who've sailed through similar contests.

Take Dana VanDen Heuvel of The Docking Station, a Green Bay, Wisconsin, coworking space. In 2009, VanDen Heuvel and his business partner entered the Northeast Wisconsin Business Plan Contest, but didn't make the short list of potential winners. Before reentering the following year, the pair contacted past winners and judges for pointers. Based on that feedback, they conducted surveys of local telecommuters on their workplace needs and compiled similar data from their chamber of commerce and area networking groups. That research became part of their second contest presentation.

"The second time around we tried to drive home that we were really innovating by bringing this to the area," VanDen Heuvel says. The effort paid off: In 2010, The Docking Station took first place, winning $10,000 and a slew of local publicity.

Hone Your Performance

Practice your pitch before an impartial audience of savvy entrepreneurs (relatives don't count). "Have your focus groups ask as many questions as they can to really try to poke holes in your idea," FlashFood's Irvin says.

Mike Grandinetti agrees. An entrepreneurship professor at Hult International Business School who has judged dozens of business plan competitions, Grandinetti calls the Q&A portion of the presentation "the most important part of the whole experience." If you can't articulate why your ideal customer or leading competitor hasn't yet solved the problem your company intends to fix, and how much customers will pay for a solution, you're probably not ready to take the stage, he says. "That's what separates the winners from the losers."

How you conduct yourself offstage carries just as much weight, according to Tabrez Ebrahim, cofounder of Evanston, Illinois–based NuMat Technologies, a clean energy technology company that has won about $1.3 million in contests, including top honors at the U.S. Department of Energy's first National Clean Energy Business Plan Competition. You're judged on every informal conversation you have—over lunch, over coffee, even while exchanging business cards in the hallway, Ebrahim says: "It's not just the 15- or 30-minute pitch session. From the moment you get there to the moment you leave, everything's important."

Inspire Confidence

Explain why you and your product are qualified to fulfill this market need. "Is it proprietary technology? Your unique background?" asks Ting, founder of Buyerly, a website that closed in 2015 that connected product manufacturers with retail buyers. Her secret sauce? Her MBA and her experience as a buyer for Target.

To hammer home the point, she offered judges an anecdote about a client who was having trouble breaking into Walmart and Target, but succeeded after using her services.

None of this is license to lie. Judges have finely tuned BS meters, Kumra notes. If you don't know the answer, say so and offer to follow up later.

Turn Up the Charm

Although judges love to see confidence, they bristle at arrogance. Contestants who become combative when challenged by the judging panel aren't doing themselves any favors and give the impression that they aren't "going to listen to my advice anyway," Parekh says.

Kunal Sarda, who was offered a $250,000 investment on TV's *Shark Tank* in 2013, agrees. "It's all about the team," says the New York–based cofounder of VerbalizeIt, an on-demand translation platform for travelers and businesses. If the judges flat out don't like you and your partners, your pitch is sunk.

Eye on Investments

Most entrepreneurs would take a no-strings cash prize over one that requires them to dilute their equity any day. But don't discount the growing number of contests that offer investment prizes outright.

Often, "when you receive a grant, the relationship ends after you get the cash," says Candace Klein, who has won 25 contests since March 2011 for a total of $500,000 in services and cash prizes. Not so with contests offering investment prizes. Klein won two equity investments in her company, Cincinnati-based SoMoLend, a business crowdfunding site, which she sold in 2013.

"They have a stake in my company," Klein says. "They're going to help give me the resources I need to be successful." Chief among them: continued introductions to more investors.

If you plan to enter contests with investment prizes, don't go it alone. Get a seasoned investor on your board of advisors who can vet such offers and consult with an attorney before signing anything. "Equity is a very scarce and precious company asset," says Mike Grandinetti. "Be sure when you sell someone equity that you are getting a fair return on it."

Looking for Competitions: The Competitive Landscape

You'll find listings of hundreds of competitions at sites like YouNoodle Compete (www.younoodle.com). Here's a sampling of the categories on offer.

- ▷ *Local competitions.* Entrepreneurial contests held by neighborhood associations and other community groups are a great place to start. You might have the hometown advantage, and you won't have to shell out cash for travel expenses.
- ▷ *The university circuit.* More than 50 U.S. universities hold contests annually, according to the Ewing Marion Kauffman Foundation. Some are so small that winners leave with nothing more than bragging rights. But bigger prizes at schools such as Rice, MIT, Stanford, and Harvard can yield significant seed money: $25,000 to $100,000.
- ▷ *Corporate contests.* Multinationals such as GE, IBM, and Microsoft have entered the competition fray. Some award five- and six-figure cash grants. Others, such as IBM's SmartCamp competition, reward winners with premier industry mentorship and networking opportunities.
- ▷ *Social entrepreneurship contests.* Entrepreneurs working on solving global problems such as hunger, poverty, energy, and education now have a smorgasbord of contests from which to choose, including the Hult Prize, which awards a $1 million prize annually.
- ▷ *Accelerators.* The real value of accelerators lies in educational and networking opportunities. MassChallenge, the granddaddy of them all, awards $1 million in cash and $10 million in in-kind prizes each year; additionally, finalists receive three months of extensive

mentoring. "One could argue that's the best prize of all," says Hult professor Mike Grandinetti.

How do you find these contests? Here are some ideas to get you started.

- www.younoodle.com
- https://www.growthink.com/businessplan/help-center/business-plan-competitions
- Business schools and incubators
- Chambers of commerce
- Economic development organizations
- Entrepreneurship organizations
- The websites of corporations that champion small businesses

Three Questions to Focus On during a Competition

When participating in a pitch competition, most entrepreneurs make the mistake of solely focusing on their pitch and neglecting to prepare for the Q&A. This can shatter your chances of taking home first place (and, more importantly, cash).

Whether you're the CEO or an intern for your company, determining the answers to the following questions will not only help you present your company in the best way possible, but it will also help you understand where your company is today and what you need to do to improve for the future. Prepare and practice for these questions, and you will blow your competition away.

Who's on Your Team?

Start off by talking about your team's experience in your market, what key skills each member brings, and why your team is the right one for the job. If you're a software company, pay special attention to your developer team, as a lot of investors want to know you have the abilities to build your product in house.

Most contestants will talk about how they have a "rock star" team and then list some impressive accomplishments (Ivy League graduates, proven track record, worked at Google, and so on). To stand out, list the additional team members you're going to need in year two and three of your venture. It makes you seem honest and mature to admit that when your startup grows to a certain point, you've already thought of your next three to four hires.

What's Your Traction to Date?

In business, "traction" refers to measurable progress or successes to date. To address traction, start with revenue if you have it—paying clients will always be a gold mine for this question. The key to answering this question is to mitigate as much risk as possible by convincing the judges you are building something that someone wants, and you need their funding to help serve your customers, who are dying for your product or service. If you're pre-revenue, beta customers are the next best thing, and if you're earlier than that, bring in how many signups you've had on your landing page.

Apart from the money or interest you're getting from your customers, this is a perfect question to tie in what you've been learning from them as well. Since a key point of the traction question is about reducing risk, talk about what traction you've made learning about what your customers want. When you can say that initially you thought X but through talking with users and tracking feedback you actually learned your users want Y and Z, you demonstrate that you've been making strides in refining your business. There are many ways to describe your traction to date, so don't underestimate the importance of all those customer interviews.

What's Your Revenue Model?

Have hard numbers here. While it may seem obvious, many teams say they are going to have annual fees, transaction fees, or premium features, but they haven't decided on the pricing yet. Also, depending on your company, be extremely careful about just listing data or advertisements as your primary revenue source. Many entrepreneurs don't understand when their data becomes valuable enough to sell, and they don't realize how many users their software needs to be self-sustaining with just ads. Be sure you have done thorough research on this point and are able to offer realistic estimates based on it.

Guy Kawasaki—marketing specialist, author, and Silicon Valley venture capitalist—once advised leaving one of the most obvious revenue options out of your answer to this question. When you omit an obvious future revenue source, many times an investor will respond with "Well, have you thought about . . ." This not only makes your company seem as though it has even more potential than you thought, but it also gets the investor to start thinking they are contributing to your team. This gets them to buy in more to your company, encourages them to keep thinking about ways to help, and, by thanking them for their suggestion, makes you seem coachable.

Pitch-Perfect: Joining Pitch Slams

You've heard of poetry slams, surely, where poets get onstage and belt out their creations in competitions that sometimes feel part stand-up comedy, part performance art. Well, slams aren't just for poets anymore—entrepreneurs compete in pitch slams, where they try to wow the judges with the best pitches. For Ash Kumra, winning a pitch slam yielded much more than the $30,000 in cash and professional services he received.

In 2010, Kumra won the Irvine Entrepreneur Forum, a pitch contest held by the chamber of commerce in Irvine, California. The win helped him launch DesiYou, a digital video distributor of Indian entertainment. Since then, he has been recognized by the White House as a young entrepreneur to watch and cofounded DreamItAlive.com, an online personal growth community with more than 50,000 members and sponsors such as Microsoft and HR provider TriNet.

Pitch slams aren't just about cash and credibility, says Kumra, who chairs the Southern California nonprofit Tech Coast Venture Network, which runs an annual $25,000 pitch contest. Win or lose, entering a contest is a clever way to meet investors and industry bigwigs with whom you couldn't otherwise rub elbows. "Contests offer instant validation," Kumra says. "That tells an investor or a sponsor that this business isn't going to disappear."

How does it work? To ensure that your pitch soars, you'll need to research the judges ahead of time, practice incessantly, and incorporate feedback from colleagues. But there are some other tips, too. Entrepreneurs who've won or run pitch slams offer the following suggestions.

Hook Them Early

"You really need to be able to convey what you do in the first 30 to 60 seconds," says Sanjay Parekh, serial technology entrepreneur and founder of Startup Riot, a twice-yearly competition in Atlanta that gives contestants three minutes to pitch and compete for startup cash and initial investor meetings.

Get Your Founding Story Out of the Way Quickly

Then share impressive sales figures, household-name customers, and industry leaders you've secured as angels or advisors, Kumra suggests. Also, he adds, mention how your business will use the winnings—whether it's to rent an office, increase inventory, or hire an engineer.

Keep It Simple

Focus your pitch on two things: identifying the problem your company solves, and how you solve it, says Los Angeles entrepreneur Vanessa Ting, who won $1,000 in a competition sponsored by Sam's Club in 2013. Make sure to quantify your market for judges who may not be familiar with your industry, she adds—for example, by saying, "160 million people in the U.S. use smartphones." Ditch the flashy props and snoozy slides, Kumra says, but by all means, demo your product.

Sometimes Publicity Is Worth More Than Cash: Q&A with Maciej Cegłowski, Founder, Pinboard Investment Co-Prosperity Cloud

Maciej Cegłowski didn't know what to expect when he announced the Pinboard Investment Co-Prosperity Cloud, a tech startup fund that emphasized publicity and mentorship rather than cash. In December 2012, more than 300 hopefuls emailed Cegłowski their startup ideas—a number the San Francisco web guru says "completely stunned" him.

In 2013, Cegłowski announced the six winners. Among them: a weather forecasting system for sailors, a web community for board game enthusiasts, and a site on which people can sell home-baked goods.

The prize? Each received $37—and a nice publicity boost and mentorship from Cegłowski, who had grown Pinboard, the social bookmarking site he launched in 2009, into a one-man, $250,000-per-year operation.

Entrepreneur asked Cegłowski about his contest.

Entrepreneur: Why $37?

Cegłowski: People need to recognize that if you have free technical labor available, you don't need additional funding for most ideas. I wanted to [test this theory] by giving a tiny token in funding, but also as much publicity as I could and as much help in getting them over the first hurdle of actually having users, whether it was access to people who could help them or introductions to potential customers. I thought the $37 would be a fun gimmick, but I was serious about trying to help people with getting the word out.

Entrepreneur: How did you choose the six winners?

Cegłowski: I had a list of criteria: Was it a viable idea for a small business? Was the person capable of building the thing they described? Did they seem like someone who had the focus to do it? It had to involve the internet so that I could, if necessary, help with introductions. I filtered out anybody who had already gotten funding or had worked on startups before, because I figured they already had a network.

Entrepreneur: How are you helping these firms?

Cegłowski: If you are trying to make an app and you get stuck and want a collaborator, I can probably help you find someone, because I have an audience that I can yell to for help. Then there's this pure psychology aspect of it: It legitimizes you. And it's not just the customer seeing you as more legitimate because you've won a contest and you're being treated like a real business. Now you start to take it seriously because someone else is taking it seriously.

Entrepreneur: *How long will these startups be under your wing?*

Cegłowski: I hope it's an indefinite relationship. In running the contest, the goal was to try to get them their first group of customers. If that turns out to make a difference in their businesses, I'll try doing another round of this.

Entrepreneur: *What is each required to do in return?*

Cegłowski: I'm out $37, so I hope to get that back someday. I'm hoping that they'll share with me what worked for them and what didn't, and that I'll hear from them down the line about how it's going. But they're not obligated to do anything. They can just take the money and run if they want.

Entrepreneur: *What do you hope to see happen with these businesses?*

Cegłowski: We have this image of startups like Facebook and the Mark Zuckerbergs of the world, where you swing for the fences, and either you get a huge hit and you're growing by hundreds of percent per year, or you fail and you try another startup. But there's so much room for these lifestyle businesses, where you actually do something for years and years and you enjoy it, and it gives you a living and independence.

Anywhere but the tech world, that's considered a wonderful victory. I want to try to remove that stigma and encourage people to actually try it. I think there's never been a better time to do it than now because of the combination of these wonderful, free online tools for building and running things and the fact that people are starting to understand that it's OK to pay 99 cents for an app or $6 for a website. It's a golden opportunity.

CHAPTER 6

Joining Incubators and Accelerators

Much like contests, pitch slams, and grants, there are hundreds upon hundreds of incubators and accelerators designed to launch the next wave of innovative startups. There are a few differences between incubators and accelerators. *Incubators* focus on developing early-stage businesses and startups, which may include things like finding office space, revving up networking, creating business plans, and yes, sometimes obtaining funding. *Accelerators* are designed to help startups grow quickly by meeting set milestones over a set period of time, normally over the course of three to six months. Accelerators provide or help arrange funding as part of their often more intense, deadline-based design.

This chapter discusses how to zero in on the programs that can best help your company, how to create the best possible application, and how to make the most of your incubation period while there.

What Corporate Incubators and Accelerators Can Mean for Your Business

With a host of companies under his belt, serial entrepreneur Rich Schmelzer launched his company, Boulder, Colorado–based GeoPalz, pretty much the only way he knew how. He bootstrapped.

But then a funny thing happened: Schmelzer met the Swoosh. Yes, that Swoosh—Nike. Schmelzer's company makes the iBitz, a personal activity monitor for kids. And when Nike announced it was launching a special accelerator for startups developing high-tech solutions that could leverage the Nike+ platform, it was serendipity.

"It literally couldn't have been a better fit," says Schmelzer, who served as CEO of GeoPalz. "I had done companies the old-fashioned way. It was time to take a different approach."

Schmelzer and his GeoPalz cofounders—his wife, Sheri, and Alexandra O'Leary—were part of a new wave of entrepreneurs launching ventures with a little help from companies that had done it before. Like renowned programs such as Y Combinator and Dreamit Ventures, these corporate-run initiatives help early- and mid-stage companies get from the concept phase through adolescence and into young adulthood. Some include capital investments; others don't. Most incorporate mentorship. All aim to foster and facilitate innovation across the board.

Why Big Companies Want In

Conceptually, these programs—once called *intrapreneurships*, a term now generally considered outdated—are not new. Think of them as incubators or accelerators, developing potentially profitable ideas and offering supportive environments for entrepreneurs, only within the confines of a big company.

Although there are no official studies, Boston-based consulting firm New Markets Advisors says a "significant" portion of Fortune 500 companies—including Procter & Gamble, IBM, Walgreens, and The

Hershey Company—likely have some sort of incubator cooking in at least one business unit.

Stephen Wunker, managing director and U.S. office head of New Markets Advisors, says that for corporations that must devote their energies to day-to-day operations and quarterly earnings, incubators offer forays into fuzzy, long-term prospects that can come into focus over time. "Given the pace of change that threatens established businesses, incubators are becoming more and more important to create growth options," he says. "For many organizations, having an internal incubator is like an insurance policy—if the market moves, the companies are ready to change directions or grow new business quickly."

Shell Global launched a corporate incubator as an offshoot of its R&D division more than 20 years ago. Dubbed GameChanger, the program is designed and run like an angel investment fund. Some accepted projects come from inside, but the incubator also evaluates proposals from universities and other outsiders—so long as the startups are focused on new initiatives involving energy.

The typical incubation period ranges from 18 to 24 months, and the average investment is $500,000. The company accepts 30 to 40 new startups per year and aims to capitalize on 10 to 20 percent of them.

"We view success as any company that secures a subsequent round of funding," Russ Conser, former manager of the GameChanger program says, noting that in some cases Shell "funds" a company itself.

There are other benefits for the companies that run these programs. They can cherry-pick projects to extend and amplify the power of their brands. They can launch new firms in their image. They can have a stake in the future.

In the case of Nike, which worked with Techstars to launch the 90-day Nike+ Accelerator in 2013, the goal was simple: to grow the Nike+ ecosystem. Dan Cherian, former general manager of Nike's Sustainable Business & Innovation Lab and current VP of Global Innovation Performance Apparel and Footwear for VF Corporation, says that, for startups, the program included relocation to Oregon for the boot camp and a host of opportunities to learn and grow.

"You don't have to do equity deals to make a difference," Cherian says. "We see participation as something bigger, something that can foster an even better relationship long-term."

Benefits for Entrepreneurs

In almost all cases, participation in a corporate incubator or accelerator enables entrepreneurs to leverage the parent company's resources to scale their business, take advantage of new technologies, and access competencies such as regulatory and/or scientific expertise that otherwise might be unavailable to independent startups.

In many instances, involvement with a corporate incubator can also mean sizable financial assistance and professional services (such as legal advice) worth big bucks. For example, companies participating in Blue Startups, an incubator from Honolulu-based Blue Planet Software, receive $20,000 in cash and a variety of professional services valued at more than $500,000.

Samantha Godfrey, cofounder of San Diego–based Pharmly, a pharmaceutical bidding marketplace, which closed in 2015, says her company benefited from mentors who gave guidance for which she would have paid top dollar had she been working on her own, as well as from $60,000 in credit for Microsoft's Azure cloud platform. "Every little bit helped," she says. "And the fact that it was all right there at our fingertips enabled us to do in three months what it would have taken us a year to complete otherwise."

There are also intangible benefits to participating in such programs. Schmelzer credits Nike+ Accelerator mentors with helping him transform GeoPalz's investor pitches. Before the tutorials, the pitches made no mention of the GeoPalz founders' previous company, Jibbitz, which made charms for Crocs shoes and eventually sold to Crocs for $20 million. After extensive critiques, Schmelzer changed the script.

"All that time I was afraid of VCs hearing about our experience with consumer goods and telling us we couldn't sell technology," he says. "The feedback helped me realize that the key takeaway was bigger than that— with Jibbitz, we built a business selling to moms and kids, and that's exactly the same audience we're trying to go after today."

In some cases, the ultimate benefit of corporate incubators is the fast track to acquisition. Wunker of New Markets Advisors likens the process to "buying a vowel" on *Wheel of Fortune.* "You're giving up a bit of your potential upside of succeeding by IPO, but you're increasing the possibility of succeeding by trade sale or in other ways," he says. "If your goal in life is to get a reasonable exit but not shoot for the moon, going into a corporate incubator might be a good approach."

It's up to you to carefully consider the pros and cons of using a corporate incubator. Some of the terms for such deals may involve potentially giving up some control of your company down the line in exchange for high-powered help getting it off the ground and up and running. More on that in the next section. You should definitely read the terms of any corporate incubator proposal very closely, and, if possible, run it past an attorney before signing on the dotted line.

Inevitable Challenges

Corporate programs are not all unicorns and rainbows. Generally they involve a lengthy application process. They can force companies to focus development on areas that benefit the parent company more than the startup itself.

In some cases, participation requires entrepreneurs to sign over a portion of equity or accept an ownership stake. There are day-to-day pitfalls, too, such as getting caught up in the politics, dysfunction, and/or bureaucracy that run rampant in large entities.

Another potential hurdle is a disconnect between the incubator and its parent company. Matt Bell, former president of Fort Worth–based GEODynamics, which manufactures equipment for the oil and gas industry, experienced this as part of Shell's GameChanger program. Bell, who graduated from the program, had capitalized on a new technology for enhancing the minerals-discovery process. But he says Shell was subsequently slow to adopt the technology, which prompted other potential users to question its usefulness.

"Ultimately we didn't get enough of an endorsement [from] the parent organization," Bell recalls. "It's great to have the name of a big company backing you, but if they don't do something with it, it can become a real problem."

Other challenges are more abstract. A number of entrepreneurs wonder about the extent to which participating in corporate incubators could be construed as "selling out." Others wonder whether industry players would be comfortable purchasing a product that was incubated by a competitor.

Venture capitalists, too, have concerns. Michael Harden, cofounder and senior partner of Artis Ventures in San Francisco, says that while he likes the concept of corporate incubators, he is "much more likely" to be skeptical of a company that has participated in one (as opposed to a traditional, stand-alone incubator or accelerator).

"If I'm investing in a company that was created and coddled by a big company early on, my presumption is that their market is going to be limited," says Harden, whose firm has invested in YouTube, Practice Fusion, and InternMatch. "I'm not saying I wouldn't invest, but I am saying I'd have a lot more questions before feeling comfortable doing so."

What to Look For

So how do you know if a particular program is right for you? According to experts and entrepreneurs who have been through them firsthand, there are a few key issues to consider.

Clearly, it's important that the program you select be focused at least somewhat on the industry you want to enter. Pharmly's Godfrey says it simply makes "good business sense" to apply for one that is—at least in some way—connected to your business. "You'll get something out of any incubator or accelerator," she says, "but you'll get more out of one designed to serve the industry you're aiming to join."

Second, you want to identify a potential friend on the inside. Wunker notes that within big organizations, people may not have the same allegiances and priorities—just because they have the same logo on their business cards doesn't mean everyone's goals will align with yours. "Ideally, you want to work with people who understand your business, appreciate how you're approaching the challenges, and, ultimately, want to see you succeed," he says. "If you can't find at least one of those advocates at a particular incubator, perhaps it's not the incubator for you."

Next, find a mentor network you can leverage. Schmelzer loves to talk about how mentors at the Nike+ Accelerator forced him and his partners to overhaul their GeoPalz business plan to focus on the lifetime value of their ustomers. His advice: Seek programs with ample and accessible mentor rosters, so you can put yourself in a position to soak up as much advice as possible.

"The great thing about an incubator is that you get to pull together all of this great advice and, if you're nimble enough, use it to change," he says. "Sometimes as entrepreneurs we get so stuck on a plan that the best thing for us to do is put ourselves in an environment that questions everything."

Finally, remember that there's no such thing as free money. Bell points out that when a corporate incubator agrees to give you funding, it comes at a cost, whether that is equity, control, or something else. If you're not open to that setup, it's better to look for programs in which no money is exchanged. "On some level, many of these relationships end up being quid pro quo," he warns. "The sooner you come to terms with that, the better off you'll be."

Accelerator Trade-Offs

The pace of growth of accelerator programs continues to rise. There are now more than 1,000 such programs in the U.S., offering early-stage startups investment and mentorship in exchange for equity.

Offering capital investment, crucial connections, advisory services, discounted resources, and investor "Demo Days" where you can pitch your business to a group of investors all at once, accelerator programs have proliferated beyond just U.S. companies. At last count, more than 1,000 such programs were in existence in the United States. Corporations like Nike and Disney have partnered with Techstars to create their own accelerator programs. Universities and even the Dubai government have done the same.

And yet, it still may not be the right move for every company. Yes, accelerators offer advantages, but they also come with some significant drawbacks, and it's important to weigh the trade-offs. These include both the cost of the equity you usually have to give away and the distractions created for your team and demands on their time.

For starters, any valuation increase may not be worth the equity you typically have to give away. Accelerator programs like Y Combinator are world-renowned for launching companies like Airbnb, Dropbox, and Stripe. There are thousands of other programs similar to Y Combinator around the world. Usually, each one takes between 3 and 7 percent of equity in a business in exchange for an investment sometimes no greater than $200,000. Founders will trade off what is usually an extremely low or discounted initial valuation for a premium from investors when they graduate.

The data backs this up to a point. Companies that progress through Y Combinator's program, for instance, can command a significant valuation increase over similar companies in the market or even those that went through other accelerator programs. Often, investors engage in pattern-matching, and the "rubber stamp" of having gone through a prestigious accelerator is viewed as a marker of potential success, even though the data doesn't necessarily support this.

But what about other accelerators that are not as prestigious as Y Combinator or 500 Startups? The data gets a lot murkier as many of the companies graduating from those other programs struggle to raise capital, and when they do, often have to do it at market rates.

Therefore, if you're considering the "valuation bump" that may come with an accelerator program, please do detailed diligence. Understand the data from previous cohorts and founders —what they raised, how long it took them to do so, and whether they would go through the program again. You may well find that the 3-to-7 percent equity isn't worth what they provide in return.

Accelerators can also cause distractions. Many accelerators mandate in-office time, attendance at programming and mentor sessions, and days of meetings in order to graduate and complete their programs. While beneficial to some founders who may be just starting out, a large percentage likewise find this programming to be a distraction.

In the early stages of a startup, founders need to be "heads down" and laser-focused on execution in shipping their product and testing their minimum viable product (MVP). Before entering an accelerator, be aware of the time commitments required and the level of distraction the program may entail. Make the decision that's right for your business.

Accelerator programs have fundamentally altered entrepreneurship. Although many business founders believe that accelerators are extraordinarily helpful or even necessary to launching their business, carefully consider that the valuation increase promised by accelerators may not be worth the required equity and the potential for distraction from core business functions.

Working with Accelerator Programs: What to Know and How to Prepare

There are a number of things a fledgling business should do when entering an accelerator program, and the following are often the best places to start:

1. **Set objectives and key results.** Some may call them key performance indicators (KPIs), but objectives and key results (OKRs) basically help a company define and prioritize its goals in an actionable, measurable way. Think of it as creating a map that sets a clear direction for employees and helps leadership mark a team's progress to a fixed destination.

   Google has relied on OKRs to set goals and track progress since the early days, in a process that involves designating an overarching goal with three to five attainable, time-bound metrics, such as improving its net promoter score or increasing organic traffic (with both tied to a target value).

   While Google establishes annual, quarterly, and short-term goals for all employees, an accelerator program doesn't have this luxury. Instead, define your startup's OKRs at the beginning of the program and then schedule weekly check-ins to mark progress.

2. **Develop a relationship with your managing director.** Accelerator managing directors get pulled in all kinds of directions during a program. They have to prioritize between helping stragglers and fueling leaders. Having a personal relationship with your managing director goes a long way toward increasing the attention and effort allocated to your company.

   Look at it this way: Only 22 percent of small businesses have mentors at their start, according to a survey by Kabbage. Managing directors can serve this role during accelerator programs. Establishing a relationship ensures your startup gets the professional guidance so many business owners don't receive when they need it the most, improving the chances of success.

3. **Establish a stretch goal.** A *stretch goal* is just as it sounds: a seemingly unattainable objective. But the beauty of something so elusive comes down to an accelerator's finite time frame, which compresses productivity—thereby changing perceptions of what's possible. You'll still be working with more practical OKRs, but a stretch goal can help push the founding team's limits.

   Besides, establishing a stretch goal can inspire and motivate employees. The seemingly unattainable objective also has a way of attracting great talent. Although you might not be in the market to hire during an accelerator, that time will come, and great people enjoy being part of a great challenge. So ask yourself, "What one thing could we do to achieve our yearly goals in six months?" And set a goal based on your answer.

4. **Understand the program's motivations.** Some accelerators seek equity value, while others hope to learn from startups. There are also those driven by partnerships or products that can be co-developed. With an influx of money from Disney, Barclays, and Microsoft, startups are suddenly finding that they have to meet corporate expectations.

   If this is your experience, get to know your funder's motives to ensure the investment is worth their time or equity. With hundreds of millions invested in startups, the companies involved will want something in return.

Accelerators are one more resource for startups to find their footing. Just understand that, like everything else in business, no program is a cure-all. You still have to put in the work to see results.

Cash and Counsel

For many startups, the initial draw of an accelerator is the potential for securing capital to refine their concept or get their business up and running. Companies can expect to receive some funding to get started or gain traction, but the amount of the stipend varies, as does the amount of equity the accelerator receives in return. Yael Hochberg, associate professor of finance and entrepreneurship at Rice University's Jones Graduate School of Business, estimates a range of 5 to 8 percent equity in return for a $15,000 to $40,000 stipend, with the median offer around 5 percent equity for a $20,000 stipend.

The money is certainly a boost, but the real draw for startups may be the exposure—to knowledge, experts, and funding—accelerators can provide. One of the marquee benefits is access to mentors who can offer experienced insight and advice in a concentrated amount of time.

"For every aspect of building the company we wanted to build, there was a specialist on hand to help us through and learn very quickly what otherwise would have taken a long time to learn," says Robert Leshner, cofounder of San Francisco–based internet-privacy protection service SafeShepherd, which was sold in 2015. His team joined Mountain View, California–based accelerator 500 Startups in October 2011. "When we needed to learn about something like SEO, there was a mentor who was incredibly knowledgeable about SEO," he explains. 500 Startups has since become the most active global investor of venture capital, making hundreds of investments every year.

Both Leshner and Bergman say they were surprised to find hat the relationships they developed with their program peers were just as valuable as the mentor connections. "Being able to speak with so many people about their experiences and bounce ideas off them is invaluable," Leshner says. "So is having this incredible network built for you of friends that you can trust."

Despite all the support, entrepreneurs still need to think for themselves. One common misconception of accelerator programs is that the advisors will give participants all the answers they need to succeed. Accelerators do provide access to informed opinions and data, but participants need to process them wisely.

"Part of the learning process is how to handle conflicting feedback from the many advisors and mentors, and trying to understand what's relevant to make their own decisions," says Jim Jen, executive director of Pittsburgh startup accelerator AlphaLab.

Ultimately it's that receptiveness to feedback that's key to getting the most out of the accelerator experience. To glean the full benefits of the program, entrepreneurs need to check their egos at the door. "It's a prestigious thing to be accepted into an accelerator, but the reality is you still haven't done anything yet," says Chris Bergman, cofounder and CEO of ChoreMonster. "If you come in thinking you're already a success, you'll miss out on learning a lot of valuable things."

Funding Is Only Part of It

The accelerator perk that gets the most headlines is access to financing information and investors. "A huge benefit for us was going through the process and understanding what raising money looks like, and all of the details of building a business with investment," Bergman says.

The potential to connect with investors—often hundreds of them—at an accelerator demo day is a huge draw, albeit one that can lead to pitfalls for participants. Hochberg says many have the mistaken perception that going through one of these programs guarantees funding at the end. "Entrepreneurs need to recognize that even 75 percent of venture-backed firms fail completely," she says. "I think sometimes that's lost on them, and it's true even at the top programs."

Focusing too much on financing was a pitfall for Leshner and his group during their time at 500 Startups. "There's a lot of investor interest for companies in the top accelerators, and that became a distraction for our team and took a lot of time away from building our company," he says. "We finally realized we should be focusing on our product instead of the money."

That's not atypical, according to Jen, whose AlphaLab minimizes discussion of financing for the first half of its program. He says such talk can lead startups to put the cart before the horse. "If they don't have the product and some early market traction, they're not going to get very far in the funding anyway," he says, "so the best thing they can do to work on their funding is work on the product."

Group Dynamics

The reality is, accelerator programs are interviewing you more than the other way around. They have the money and expertise, and as long as you read the fine print about what they want, to some extent they are interchangeable. What do they want? A strong team is everything. With acceptance rates to some of the country's top-tier accelerators hovering around 1 percent, a standout application is integral to getting one's foot in the door. Of course, pitching the product and the market it serves is important, but insiders agree that portraying a strong business team is even more crucial.

"In addition to your product, you're also being judged on your team," says Hochberg. "Your idea or product can change quite a bit as you go through the program, in terms of the business model or even what exactly you'll be producing, so there's also a lot of evaluation of the team and whether there's a sense that you fit together well, understand the challenges ahead of you, and will be able to be successful entrepreneurs."

Jen says the capabilities of the team need to come out during the application process. "A lot of it is convincing them that as a team you have the passion, the commitment, and the drive to make this company happen no matter what," he says. "Then you need to show you have the capabilities to execute on what you want to do."

The same is true at the end of the program, on demo day. "Communicating a sense of your team and why you're capable of being successful is much more important than communicating the details of your product," says Leshner. "Your product or idea is likely to evolve, but the team is a constant."

Choose Wisely

Jen defines a true accelerator as a time-specific, mentorship-driven program designed to provide startups with critical resources to help them make rapid progress on product and customer development. "There are a lot of incubators and shared working spaces that are incorporating a lot of the elements of accelerators, but it's a smaller universe that applies to the definition of a true accelerator, and even a smaller number that have been around and have a proven track record," says Jen.

Hochberg also has concerns about the legitimacy of some accelerators. She fears that not all programs, particularly the newer ones, can deliver on their promises of offering high-quality mentorship, network introductions, and exposure to the capital community.

"To help founders, you have to be very good at screening so that you're only taking in groups that really have a chance of succeeding. And I'm not convinced that all of the accelerators out there are equipped to do that,"

Hochberg says. In addition, she points out, there are only a finite number of great mentors to go around.

Quality funding sources are also a concern. It's important to verify that an accelerator can bring valid investors to the table. "With the top programs, everybody in the VC community will be looking at you," Hochberg says. "But with some of these newer accelerators, especially regional ones or those in nontraditional verticals, you need to be sure that serious VC shops from outside your area take the program seriously and see its alumni as serious possibilities for funding."

For assurance about any of these issues, due diligence is key. Applicants should conduct thorough research online and talk to past participants to verify exactly who is involved in the program, what kinds of connections they have, and how many of the accelerator's alumni have received funding and at what stage.

Besides top-tier programs like Y Combinator, Techstars, and 500 Startups, there are lots more to check out and apply to. You can always search the web, as the startup scene is constantly changing. But a good place to start might be the list by Sergio Paluch at Beta Boom, updated to 2023. It's a ranking by exit rate, or the percentage of companies who exit the program successfully, typically by being acquired, going public, or achieving financial independence by no longer needing the accelerator's services. Some of its top-rated accelerators include AngelPad, Stanford's StartX, Microsoft Accelerator, and Google Launchpad Accelerator. Of course, you want to deeply research whichever accelerators seem attractive to you.

Making sure an accelerator is a good fit for your business is also important. "If you're a health-care startup, it doesn't matter if they're the best consumer internet VCs on the planet and the mentors are all consumer internet gurus; if you're doing health care, that's not the right fit for you," Hochberg says.

With the pool of accelerators expanding daily, doing the research and making decisions can be tricky, but it is crucial to choosing the program that will benefit your business the most. "Equity is an extremely precious thing to be handing away," Hochberg points out. "You need to make sure that you're handing it away to an organization that will truly be able to help you."

Q&A with Aigerim Shorman: Jump-Starting Your Business with an Accelerator Program

Making connections was priority number one for Aigerim Shorman and Shana Zheng. As founders of Triptrotting, a community that connected travelers with locals both online and with the Wist app, the pair quickly recognized that startup accelerators could be their ticket to mentorship and funding.

After raising $300,000 in seed money from Pasadena, California, incubator Idealab and launching their company, Shorman and Zheng applied to Launchpad LA, the Los Angeles accelerator program founded by venture capitalist Mark Suster. Launchpad invests between $25,000 and $100,000 in each company accepted into its four-month program and provides business advice, free shared office space, and networking opportunities.

Through this program, Triptrotting raised nearly $1.5 million more from investors such as GV (formerly Google Ventures) and 500 Startups. *Entrepreneur* spoke with Shorman about her adventures in fundraising:

Entrepreneur: *Why did you apply to Launchpad?*

Shorman: We wanted access to more mentors and more investors. Launchpad was one of the big up-and-coming accelerators in Santa Monica, which is becoming an entrepreneurial center here in Los Angeles. We wanted to be at the heart of it. We thought it would be a great opportunity for us to meet people and expand our network.

Entrepreneur: *What was the application process like?*

Shorman: There's an application you fill out on the Launchpad website. You need to have an elevator pitch, a business model, and a distribution and marketing plan. They had more than 400 applications for this class. For the final round, we met with managing director Sam Teller and had dinner. Then we got our invitation to join.

Entrepreneur: How has the program helped you with networking?

Shorman: They have a speaker series on Monday evenings that really gives us great exposure to successful entrepreneurs, investors, and mentors. Everything becomes part of this environment. Even sitting in the open office space, people come in and out every day, and we meet hundreds of people.

Entrepreneur: So investors just waltz in looking for hot startups to fund?

Shorman: Pretty much. The whole idea of the program is to get companies funded. It's very bright and open. There are no walls. Most of the conversations happen more or less in open space. Investors sometimes meet with companies right at their desk, after the introductions are made.

We were already fundraising when we joined Launchpad, so it was much easier to talk to investors who came in. And some of our investors—[GV], for example—didn't come to Launchpad, but we met them through an introduction.

Entrepreneur: What are the other benefits of being part of an accelerator?

Shorman: The mindset. The caliber of people you're surrounded by makes you realize how much further you could be going and how much you can achieve. You become part of this environment that's trying to make bold moves. Everyone helps each other out. We will always say, "Hey, what do you think about this splash page? What do you think about this design?"

Entrepreneur: What advice can you give others interested in accelerator programs?

Shorman: Obviously, you have to have a great business model and a great idea. But it's also important to have a cohesive team driving the business. High-quality accelerators like Launchpad want teams that are dedicated. People like Suster and Teller can tell if you are just playing around at this or if you are serious.

Corporate Incubators

What's the difference between accelerators and incubators? When should you pursue one type over the other?

Both types of programs provide guidance to startups and help advance their business models and strategies, and the main goal is to groom the startup to become valuable in the eyes of investors. However, key differences exist between accelerators and incubators. When examining the selection and investment process, the differentiation between the two becomes more apparent.

Purpose

Incubators support startups entering the beginning stages of building their company. The startups possess an idea to bring to the marketplace, but little or no business model and direction to transition from innovative idea to reality. *Accelerators* advance the growth of existing companies that have an idea and business model in place. These programs build upon the startups' foundations to catapult them forward to investors and key influencers.

Duration

Incubators operate on an open-ended timeline. They focus more on the longevity of a startup and are less concerned with how quickly the company grows. It is not uncommon for incubators to mentor startups for more than a year and a half. Accelerators operate on a set time frame, which usually lasts three to four months. During this period, startups build out their business with the support of mentors and capital provided by the accelerator. At the end of the program, startups receive the opportunity to pitch their businesses to investors.

Application Process

Incubators invest time and resources into advancing local startups; they are generally tasked with creating jobs or finding ways to license intellectual property. Startups are a conduit to accomplish both. Incubators have less pressure to deliver startups that can grow fast, as fostering and supporting local startups is part of their charter. Therefore, even a slow growing or less scalable business constitutes a good incubator candidate. Accelerators use a more traditional and formal model for entry into their program. Participants must apply for a select number of slots in the program. These programs are extremely competitive as the accelerator must select the top startups from across the country, which are scalable and investable and have to show an ability to grow rapidly within months.

Environment

Both incubators and accelerators offer an environment of collaboration and mentorship. This enables the startups to share a space, as well as have access to a multitude of resources and peer feedback. Both also provide mentorship from seasoned entrepreneurs and business experts.

Investment capital

Incubators do not traditionally provide capital to startups and are often funded by universities or economic development organizations. On the other hand, they also don't usually take an equity stake in the companies they support. Accelerators do invest a specific amount of capital in startups in exchange for a predetermined percentage of equity. Due to this investment, the accelerators bear a greater responsibility in the success of the startup.

When deciding which program is right for your startup, you should look at your situation and consider which would be the better fit. Most startups could benefit from being in an incubator, but fewer are a fit for an accelerator. Incubators tend to take on startups that are still in formation, may not necessarily require investment capital, and tend to be part of the local startup community already. The timeline to commercialization may be longer, or they are so early that some of the basics have not been addressed yet.

Accelerators have national calls to apply and pick from among hundreds of pre-vetted applicants. These startups must be able to demonstrate they are investible and rapidly scalable businesses willing to relocate to the town where the accelerator is housed for at least the duration of the program. The accelerator fund will be the startup's first outside investor in most cases. While both programs provide significant benefits to startups, they are not to be considered one and the same. Through careful self-reflection, entrepreneurs will be able to determine which is the right fit for their business at that moment.

Example Incubator Story: Simple & Crisp

For Jane Yuan, the owner of Seattle-based Simple & Crisp, an order from Whole Foods Market to sell her dried-fruit crackers nationally was the opportunity of a lifetime. But she didn't have the money to buy two additional dehydrators at $17,000 a pop, which she'd need to scale up and fill that order as well as those from her other customers. "That became a cash-intensive launch," Yuan says, "and being a small business, we didn't have access to capital that quickly."

So she turned to Whole Foods' loan program, borrowing $37,000 for five years at 5 percent interest. That was in 2014. She took a second loan from the retailer in 2015 for $50,000 at the same terms. Today, Simple & Crisp products sell in approximately 300 Whole Foods stores, as well as 100 other grocery and specialty food shops nationwide.

Whole Foods isn't the only household name to offer small business loans or grants. Martha Stewart Living, Miller Lite, FedEx, Chase, and Wells Fargo have all awarded from $10,000 to $200,000 in grants to select small businesses in recent years.

It's not just about money, though. The PR boost that comes with landing brand-sponsored cash can put a small company on the business-media map. "You gain a lot of [recognition] from winning. It's huge," says Mary Lynn Schroeder, CEO of In Blue Handmade, the Asheville, North Carolina, leather crafting business that took the $25,000 grand prize in FedEx's small business grant contest in 2015.

The mentorship and networking opportunities can be just as valuable. Take Whole Foods, which finds and mentors promising suppliers to get their products and packaging shelf-ready, often before awarding them a loan. Some programs send grantees to a brand-sponsored summit, where winners swap advice and war stories. To Schroeder, the trip to FedEx's 2015 small business summit, where she and fellow winners "think-tanked it out," was invaluable.

Before applying for these loans or grants, make sure the brand's program is a good fit. Denise Breyley, retired Principal Forager of Whole Foods, points out that Whole Foods sells only products that shun artificial ingredients and meet certain sustainability and animal-welfare standards. Plus, the company provides loans only for equipment and other fixed assets, not for "soft costs" such as marketing campaigns.

Some incubators are nearly as competitive as accelerators and involve judges who choose from online submissions. For grants with an online voting component, such as those offered by FedEx and Martha Stewart's company, you'll need more than a compelling, well-honed business plan and proven customer base. You'll also need a strong web presence. In other words, get comfortable sharing photos, videos, and the personal details of your business journey on social media, because judges eat that up.

"You have to put yourself out there a little bit," says Becky Huling, FedEx's vice president of customer engagement marketing. "You're really trying to create an emotional connection with the people who are selecting the contest winners."

To stand out from the crowd, tell your story with authenticity and personality. "You need to explain who you are and how you got there," Schroeder says. "Because every small business has a lot of heart, and you need to let that shine through."

Inside the Big Guns: Dos and Don'ts of Y Combinator and Techstars

Accelerators are an amazing way for entrepreneurs to learn the ropes of launching (and running) a business while also gaining valuable connections. That is, if the founders select the right one for their needs. Participating in the Techstars Boston accelerator program has had a profound effect on the success of Moritz Plassnig's company Codeship, a developer-tool business. In this section, he gives some smart advice on using elite accelerators like Y Combinator and Techstars.

"I made vital connections, expanded my local network, received excellent advice, and increased my work ethic due to long hours of training sessions, demonstration preparations, and mentorship meetings," he says. "By the time my team and I graduated from the program, we had attracted local investors and were on our way to receiving our Series A funding. This probably wouldn't have happened if it hadn't been for Techstars, and I'm grateful I had the opportunity. But all accelerator programs are not created equal."

Here's how to make sure you get the most out of yours:

❯ *DO consider the big picture.* A big name like Y Combinator or Techstars isn't everything, as these accelerators may not make sense for your company's vision. That said, it's important to work with an organization that already has an established network in your desired location.

"For example, I knew I wanted to relocate my business from Vienna, Austria, to Boston, so I made sure to look at programs in that area. If you finish the program and then move somewhere totally new, you can't take that local network with you. Before you apply, do your homework. Find out the names of the people heading up the program and consider their background and areas of expertise. Do they have a lot of experience in an area you need to improve to grow your business? Are they a financier who has invested in a company like yours before? Think about it, and make an educated decision based on the whole package."

❯ *DON'T expect fun and games.* "Participating in Techstars was one of the most rewarding—and taxing—times in my life. My cofounders and I were new to Boston and excited to join a fresh community where a lot of the people were just like us—young entrepreneurs entering the tech-startup scene. But there was little time to explore and check out the area once we arrived."

Most accelerator programs last several weeks—or sometimes months—and require jam-packed schedules filled with intense mentorship sessions, presentations, and a demo day. You won't have a lot of free time. Be ready for that.

❯ *DO leverage the network.* Think about how the people involved in the program can help you, and always have your elevator pitch ready. Hit the pavement running and get customers. Make sure your MVP (Most Viable Product) is ready. Show the people around you that you're able to build a company and that you're already well on your way. They'll be more likely to take a chance on you when you're done with the program and looking for funding.

❯ *DON'T wait for other people to do your work.* Though the program will definitely be educational, it's not school, so don't expect your "teachers" to nag you to get your work done. An accelerator program can be a great opportunity, but you'll only get out of it what you put into it. Find inspiration by focusing 100 percent on your company and envisioning its success. It's yours. Make the decisions. Build the business. At the same time, don't be afraid to ask for help. Ask the hard questions.

> *DO have clear, defined roles within your team.* Make sure everyone knows the part they have to play. There's only one CEO—not everyone will be doing the pitching. Your marketing person should be learning how to build your brand, and your product developer should be talking to customers and focusing on building a product the market really needs. You, as CEO, need to make sure you're in front of the right people telling your story. Everyone has a different, but equally important, role that will contribute to the overall success of the company.

> *DON'T waste time.* You have to wake up every day determined to win. You've been given one big chance to make your dream a reality, and it will be over in the blink of an eye. Savor every moment and listen carefully to every piece of advice you receive. Once you "graduate," another class will take your place, and you and your team will be history. Make the most out of your time and demand not to be forgotten.

Niche Incubators and Accelerators

The U.S. has become rich with new incubators and accelerators aimed at startups in such categories as art and design, biotech, music, cannabis, social enterprises, clean energy, and artificial intelligence. This section covers what you need to know about some of these programs.

(A number of incubation and acceleration programs aimed at social impact businesses and women- and minority-led startups are covered in Chapters 7, 9, and 10.)

Art and Design: NEW INC

Artists and designers have long been underserved by traditional tech incubators. "Scaling may not be their first priority," says Julia Kaganskiy, director of NEW INC, an incubator run by the New Museum in New York City. For example, she says, rather than solving a widespread problem, technology-minded artists may want to create a product that's simply playful or makes a statement.

NEW INC gives artists, designers, and technologists a place to build products, design studios, and web development shops. The program offers qualifying entrepreneurs full-time annual memberships or part-time three- to six-month terms, both renewable, with space available for 100 members. Artists retain all equity in their businesses and all intellectual property rights to their work.

Allison Wood joined NEW INC in 2014 to get her startup off the ground. "I think about it as my creative MBA," says the co-creator and CEO of Reify, a platform that turns music into sculptures using 3-D technology and augmented reality. "It was my first time starting a business, and I knew I needed to be somewhere that I had the creative support as well as the professional development support to make it work."

To accommodate its range of members, NEW INC teaches fundraising tactics, from grant writing and crowdfunding to angel investments and venture capital. Demo-day audiences include investors, gallery curators, creative directors from top brands and agencies, and members of the press.

Collaboration is encouraged. Wood met her company's CTO, creative director, art director, and several freelance designers through NEW INC. "It's been pretty awesome to have all that under one roof," says Wood, who now rents a second office in Brooklyn for her growing team. "I don't think you can pay for that."

Biotech: The BioScience Center

At The BioScience Center, an incubator for biotech and life science startups in Albuquerque, New Mexico, entrepreneurs are encouraged to stay for at least three years. "Biotech has a little bit longer runway," says Lisa Adkins, COO and director of the center, which launched in 2013. "It takes them longer to get going and certainly to get funded and to get to proof of concept and whatever sort of testing they need to do." Not to mention, she adds, to get through the protracted FDA approval process.

For founders on this path, the 20,000-square-foot center provides offices and wet chemistry and microbiology labs at below-market rates; alternatively, founders can exchange a small percentage of their equity or future revenue for use of the space. Either way, the package includes an assortment of industry mentors, workshops, and mock pitch sessions. The Center focuses on affordable space, funding leads, shared resources, laboratories, and networking and learning opportunities.

For Rodney Herrington, an engineer who invented a handheld water purifier, the avalanche of information he received at the Center has been priceless. The same goes for the referrals to manufacturers, investors, and other potential partners his incubator colleagues routinely share.

"There are people in the building who are saying, 'Since you're looking for financing, here's another angel investor you might be interested in.' That's quite valuable," notes Herrington, whose H2gO Purifiers now sell at REI and other sporting goods stores as well as to nongovernmental organizations offering assistance in developing countries.

Music: Project Music

You can't build a game-changing music technology company without understanding the intricacies of the industry and the specific concerns of artists and executives. (Witness the demise of streaming music service Grooveshark, shuttered in 2015 over a copyright lawsuit.) That's the philosophy behind Project Music, a boot camp for idea-stage music-tech startups piloted by The Nashville Entrepreneur Center in Tennessee.

"Music-minded entrepreneurs have unique needs," says Vice President of Operations Heather McBee, noting that the business is complex, networking is tough for outsiders, and, unless you go to a college with a program focused on the industry, "there isn't an easy way to get an education."

Project Music includes intensive sessions with insiders who share details on A&R, licensing, publishing, distribution, and marketing, along with the expected tech curriculum of prototyping, customer acquisition, and fundraising, says McBee, a 20-plus-year veteran of the music industry.

Members receive hands-on mentorship, desks in the Entrepreneur Center, and $30,000 in seed money in exchange for 10 percent equity.

Investors get a sneak peek at the ventures halfway through the program, and the camp culminates with demo days in Nashville and New York.

The eight startups in the pilot program—selected from an international pool of 90 applicants—have since raised more than $2 million in private investments. They include a platform for selling classical music online, another for artists to find collaborators, and an app that improves the sound quality of streaming music based on a user's personal "hearing profile."

For Stephen Davis, cofounder of the hearing app Ear.IQ, Project Music was a networking gold mine. Among Ear.IQ's spoils: a letter of intent from a major auto manufacturer interested in buying his product and board members ranging from a former Shazam executive to a doctor of audiology.

"I managed to get more accomplished and made more contacts in 14 weeks than I did in an entire year working from home," Davis says.

Cannabis: Green Labs

Startups in the legal marijuana business have unique concerns—initially, finding a bank, credit card provider, and landlord. Even those who don't grow, sell, or process the plant face obstacles most entrepreneurs don't have to deal with. It's no surprise, then, that incubators serving pot startups have cropped up nationwide to help.

Green Labs Denver is an incubator and coworking space for ancillary cannabis businesses, such as apps, vending machines, and tourism.

"We're all facing the same legislative hurdles," says Green Labs cofounder Mike Looney. The way he sees it, startups in this volatile industry stand a better chance at success by banding together and pooling their resources.

Green Labs' incubation arm makes equity investments in high-growth-potential startups, Looney says. Besides providing free desk space and business services, the Green Labs team coaches startups on revenue models, sales strategy, and investor pitches. Also included: introductions to private investors and free legal advice from attorneys in Green Labs' extended network.

Further upping the networking ante are Green Labs' community events, hosted throughout the month (examples: Yoga and Cannabis, and Sushi and Joint Rolling). But during business hours it's all work and no blaze. "It's people on their laptops all day," Looney says. "It's a very upscale space, and we want to keep it that way."

Social Enterprises: Halcyon Incubator

Brian Ferguson was wrongfully convicted of first-degree murder and imprisoned for 11 years. After his release in 2013, he and brother Albert Ferguson began developing Start Line (originally called Angel's List), a comprehensive database of available employment, housing, health care, and other social services for prisoners returning to life on the outside.

Brian, who was handed a list of outdated resources upon his release, saw the need firsthand. "There was no hub," Albert explains. So the pair hatched an idea to build one online.

It was just the kind of venture that Halcyon Incubator—a Washington, D.C.–based residential fellowship for social entrepreneurs—was looking for.

"We wanted to find the most talented entrepreneurs that we could, tackling the most hairy 21st-century social problems in the most courageous and innovative ways," says Kate Goodall, COO of S&R Foundation, the nonprofit that funds Halcyon, which launched in the fall of 2014.

Halcyon fellows receive a $10,000 stipend and live and work at Halcyon in D.C. for 14 weeks. They gain lifelong contacts and are showered with training and resources.

The program has an emphasis on personal, professional, and project diversity. All fellows receive a dedicated mentor in their field, be it solar energy or child malnutrition, plus a leadership coach with whom they can discuss doubts and personal issues they may not want to share with their business mentor. They also receive free PR, marketing, legal, and accounting help courtesy of Halcyon's partnerships with companies like Deloitte and KPMG.

At the end of the residency, venture capitalists, angel investors, and philanthropists attend the program's demo day. More than 90 percent of Halcyon's fellows have raised funds from outside investors, Goodall says, adding that the incubator does not take a cut of the businesses incubated.

"It's the social good that they're investing in," Albert Ferguson says. "That, to me, is just phenomenal."

Clean Energy: Greentown Labs

In late 2010, four energy entrepreneurs pooled their resources for an affordable Boston-area warehouse space where they could build hardware prototypes. Today that collective has ballooned into Greentown Labs— 40,000 square feet of office, event, and machine-shop space that incubates nearly 50 energy and clean technology startups.

In addition to workspace, members get shared machine-shop tools, free software licensing, and access to hardware such as 3-D printers. "They basically get about $130,000 in resources," says Greentown Labs CEO Emily Reichert. And that's not including the benefit of working alongside dozens of engineers who can help troubleshoot in a pinch.

Educational workshops and one-on-ones cover topics like manufacturing, marketing, scaling overseas, intellectual property, and government funding and contracts. Exposure to angel, VC, and corporate investors is ongoing, with financiers periodically visiting from as far as Silicon Valley and an annual demo day attracting roughly 250 attendees, Reichert says.

Silverside Detectors, which develops nuclear radiation detection technology, joined Greentown Labs in 2013 after winning two prizes in a prestigious startup competition. The company needed a place to build and test prototypes, but it couldn't shoulder the burden of a long-term commercial lease and accompanying overhead, says Sarah Haig, cofounder and COO.

"It's a Catch-22," Haig explains. "You need a prototype in order to get any sort of funding. But you need funding in order to get space where you can prototype. So Greentown Labs was a godsend."

In 2021, Greentown Houston opened, a 40,000-foot incubator that serves 200 startups dedicated to transitioning from fossil fuels to sustainable energy.

Artificial Intelligence: Analytics Ventures

With the introduction of OpenAI's GPT large language models and its ChatGPT chatbot, the long-anticipated AI revolution seems to have finally begun. Heavyweights like Google, Meta, and Microsoft are scrambling to achieve dominance in this sphere. But startups also hope to make breakthroughs and find new applications for artificial intelligence in products and services. The atmosphere is reminiscent of the emergence of the World Wide Web in the 1990s—it's a land grab, a gold rush, whatever you want to call it, and loads of money are being poured into this suddenly red-hot tech space. As of the time of writing, investors are eager to get in on the ground floor of just about anything to do with AI.

Naturally, incubators and accelerators have popped up focusing on supporting AI startups. For example, Analytics Ventures matches up investors and AI researchers and entrepreneurs. Its AV Fund in particular seeks to provide AI-focused businesses with the resources they need to gain a foothold in this fast-moving technology area.

As the company says, "Each venture goes through a highly controlled and accountable formation framework that provides the highest level of predictability and accountability from inception through market launch. Being a fund that starts new AI-enabled businesses, our overall objective is to build industry disrupting ventures that are being validated via a public, revenue generating market launch as quickly and efficiently as possible, often within a six-month period. We are fast, agile, and have a proven execution model that allows everybody to focus on what's needed to incubate, validate, and launch innovative AI-based businesses."

Projects so far have included nurturing startups in the health-care industry, including specialties such as diagnostics and treatment, plus sustainable energy, distributed digital workload processing, advertising, and stock trading. The company's lab is staffed by data scientists and specialists in neuroscience, machine learning, and systems theory to fuel artificial intelligence applications. In other words, if you have an idea to use AI to create or improve a product or service, Analytics Ventures and many similar incubators aim to help bring it to fruition.

Looking Beyond American Shores for Incubators and Accelerators

By the time he was a senior at the University of Wisconsin in 2009, Nathan Lustig's startup had customers, revenue, and national press. But the company, a digital estate-planning service called Entrustet, lacked a scalable business model and had yet to turn a profit.

That's when Lustig and his cofounder, Jesse Davis, made a bold move. Presented with an opportunity to join Start-Up Chile, a program the Chilean government launched in 2010 to attract entrepreneurs to the country, they leaped at the chance. Under the program, Lustig received $40,000 in equity-free capital, a one-year work visa, office space in Santiago, and a steady stream of introductions to the country's business elite, including potential investors and partners.

"We probably couldn't have gotten $40,000 of free money in the U.S.," says Lustig, who raised $125,000 in equity funds from friends, family, and angels in the U.S. before moving to Chile.

Lustig sold Entrustet to a European competitor in 2012 but remains in Santiago, where he cofounded Magma Partners, a $5 million seed investment fund and accelerator for local and expat entrepreneurs doing business in Chile. And he is not alone: An increasing number of financing opportunities exist for U.S. businesspeople willing to move overseas, courtesy of governments, private companies, seed funds, accelerators, and incubators seeking savvy startups.

A Capital Idea

"Around the world, people look up to entrepreneurs in the U.S. as being on the cutting edge of technology and innovation," says Nancy Yamaguchi, a partner at international law firm Withers Worldwide. This reputational advantage can open doors to foreign VCs, strategic investors, and other financiers, says Yamaguchi, who works with tech companies raising capital overseas.

Besides competing with fewer startups for dough, another benefit of looking abroad is that overhead may be significantly cheaper—as much as 50 percent less than in the U.S., according to Evan Tann, a native Californian who spent six months at Wayra, a London-based accelerator run by $100 billion Spanish telecom giant Telefónica. "Even in London, where living costs are significantly more expensive than the U.S., engineers charge a small fraction of their San Francisco counterparts," says Tann, CEO of Cloudwear and now the cofounder and CEO of About Labs.

New Worlds, New Networks

Your eventual goal might be to find VC funds overseas, and if so, a faster way to get there may be to align yourself with an overseas accelerator. Making the connections needed to raise angel or VC funds overseas can take time. Californian Kevin Yu, founder of the mobile cooking app SideChef, spent a year raising a $1 million seed round in Shanghai. Even though he spoke Mandarin, Yu understood the business culture and the importance of having a local friend make introductions.

Aligning oneself with an overseas accelerator or incubator that offers capital—such as London's Innovate Finance, Italy's M31, or Shenzhen's HAX Accelerator—is more expedient, according to Yamaguchi. "I like the incubators because they are a clearinghouse for local VC resources," the attorney says, adding that international programs provide more access to investors than their U.S. counterparts. Tann concurs, saying that, at Wayra, "there was a constant stream of investors through the office."

But don't just follow the money blindly, Lustig warns. Those willing to take the plunge to move overseas should carefully weigh the potential markets, where they can afford to set up shop, and—most important— where they want to live. "If you're going to go abroad," he says, "it should be for a reason, not just for the cash."

Expat Resources

For help building a business abroad, you need to know more than local museum hours. One place to start is the U.S. Chamber of Commerce, which details information on regional chambers abroad; you should also check out trade and industry organizations in your regions of interest (such as the Japan External Trade Organization, or JETRO) and overseas accelerators and incubators (such as Start-Up Chile and Italy's M31). Here are two startup-friendly resources that can help get you started:

> » *Nomad List* (nomadlist.com) is a global community of international remote workers, offering a filterable ranking of worldwide cities, based on cost of living, internet speed, weather, and other criteria.
> » *The Tropical MBA* (www.tropicalmba.com) is a long-running podcast and blog about starting a business anywhere in the world.

CHAPTER 7

Crowdfunding Like a Champ

Crowdfunding has become a proven way to test-market interest for your product or service, get media coverage for your idea (should your financing campaign go viral), and show investors you've done the fundraising legwork long before you show up to pitch them. As of 2022, more than $30 billion has been raised through crowdfunding platforms worldwide. This chapter covers how to mount the most successful crowdfunding campaign you can.

Crowdfunding is the process of raising money to fund a project or business venture through many donors using an online platform, such as Kickstarter, Indiegogo, or

Crowdfunder. The fundraising window is usually finite—90 days, for instance—and fees and rules vary across platforms.

Crowdfunding allows the fundraiser to set up a public campaign for accepting donations. The campaign will advertise details such as the nature of the project or venture, the amount of money the company is hoping to raise, and the campaign's fundraising deadline. People can donate a specified amount through the fundraising campaign's website and often receive some sort of acknowledgment or reward in return for their donation. Some crowdfunding platforms use a share-selling model, meaning donors receive shares in the startup in return for donations. It is of course important to determine the appropriate model for your business when choosing a platform.

Campaigns can range from charitable and educational projects to creative projects like films, as well as campaigns to support scalable businesses. Crowdfunding platforms tend to cater to specific categories; Kickstarter, for example, focuses on creative projects, while Crowdfunder is an equity-based platform used by businesses looking to raise investment capital. SeedInvest Technology specializes in bringing donors together with startups. The process involves an application and vetting process, and the platform takes a 5 percent equity and charges a 7.5 percent placement fee.

Overwhelmingly, crowdfunding campaigns do not meet their fundraising goals. Around three out of four projects—depending on the platform—fail to reach their funding targets before the end date, according to a report from London-based market research firm The Crowdfunding Center.

To be sure, there are a smattering of factors that contribute to the success or failure of a crowdfunding campaign. For example, Kickstarter has all-or-nothing fundraising rules, meaning that if the established crowdfunding goal is not met, donations are returned to backers and the campaign owner walks away with nothing. That's motivation to hustle hard.

Other platforms, such as Indiegogo, have a flexible-funding option so that no matter what percentage of the fundraising goal is reached, the campaign backer still gets the money minus a 9 percent fee. Other factors affecting the success or failure of a crowdfunding campaign, such as how visual the page is and how far ahead of time the owner starts promoting the campaign, have nothing to do with the platform that is hosting the campaign.

The power of crowdfunding comes from the accumulation of a large number of small donations from backers. In this way it is the opposite concept behind venture capital and incubator models, where one or a handful of financial backers provide most of the funding in exchange for a stake in the startup should it become successful.

The takeaway for anyone looking to raise funds on one of these platforms is: You're not depending on a small number of donors to lay down the big bucks to get your campaign to the finish line. Instead, you are spreading the word of your crowdfunding campaign far and wide in hopes of getting lots and lots of smaller pledges.

Nine Steps to Launching a Successful Crowdfunding Campaign

Some of the most successful crowdfunding campaigns include the Coolest Cooler, which raised more than $13 million—or 26,570 percent of its original funding goal—and Exploding Kittens, which amassed just under $9 million, or 87,825 percent of its initial funding goal. If a multi-function cooler / blender / music player and a card game about kittens and explosions can exceed their funding goals by such large margins, imagine what you could do with your revolutionary and innovative business idea.

This isn't to suggest that crowdfunding campaigns are easy. However, the good news is that launching a successful crowdfunding campaign can essentially be broken down into the following nine steps.

Share Your Story

Let your potential funders know how your product or business idea can benefit them or a community they may care about, or society or the economy. In your written story that appears on your campaign, share who you are, what you're planning to do, where the project idea came from, what your budget is, and why you're passionate about it. Doing so shows you've actually put some thought into the idea, which helps prove the legitimacy and credibility of your project and instantly lifts you beyond other campaigns that put little thought into this presentation.

An outline of this information will be available at just about any crowdfunding site. Reading as much as you can about the most successful strategies found by each site is essential. Consider it homework that can literally pay off.

Communicating your story through attractive visual imagery and design principles is of particular importance. Make sure to create a great-looking project header image as well as a compelling video. Video is particularly important, and can even make or break your project.

Ensure that your video is professional-looking. Most campaigns that do well in crowdfunding have high-quality videos. Make it engaging and fun to watch, and don't cut corners with the production. Make sure the video quality is crystal clear, your story is compelling, and your product shines. Show you are credible by speaking clearly, outlining the concept and the benefits, and demonstrating exactly how it works. Connect emotionally with a personal story in a way that a potential backer will be able to relate to. Finally, talk about why the product is unique. People need to know what problem you're solving that will be appealing to consumers.

Most people make decisions based on a feeling, long before they have a rational reason to do so. This is why your pitch needs to encourage people to have an emotional investment in you and your product. This applies to crowdfunding for absolutely anything, including movies, products, services, music, and social causes. There are thousands upon thousands of other campaigns competing for the support of the same people you want to back your idea.

According to Thomas Alvord, cofounder of Funded Today, a consulting company for crowdfunding campaigns:

> *"We often overlook that Kickstarter and Indiegogo are social networks. It's more than just the product. It's also about the creator, the creation process, and being part of a sub-crowd that brings a product to life.*
>
> *"In business generally, consumers can connect more with a person than with the brand (think Steve Jobs). This is even more true in crowdfunding. Consumers don't have a finished product to*

analyze in a crowdfunding campaign. Consequently, consumers are also evaluating who the creator is and what type of product a given creator is capable of making, whether they realize it or not.

"Many crowdfunding campaigns are for products that solve pain points that creators themselves experienced, then went and solved. When creators can share their personal story of pain and then their solution, consumers can see themselves in the creators' shoes and are much more likely to pledge."

Offer Great Rewards

People will back your project if they think it's worthwhile, but it's always good to have great perks for your pledgers, too.

Most crowdfunding platforms have limitations on what can be offered to donors. For example, Kickstarter's Creator Handbook spells out what you can and cannot offer, as there are some restrictions you'll need to be aware of. You'll also want to be fair with your rewards in terms of price points, and make sure you can actually fulfill them.

It's fine to promise your pledgers big rewards, but don't forget that delivery can take considerable time and effort. Be realistic.

Set a Funding Goal

If you're launching your campaign on a platform like Kickstarter, be aware of the all-or-nothing funding model. If you meet or exceed your funding goal, you get to keep the money. If not, you don't get anything, and the pledges are returned to the donors. Of course, platforms such as Indiegogo work on a slightly different model, where you can choose to keep the partially successful funding regardless of whether you reach your goal.

Consider how much money you'll really need to get your business up and running, and how many people you know who would be willing to pledge. Although you may attract the attention of new people with your campaign, most of your support is going to come from those who already know you. So be realistic.

Also keep in mind that you can't change your funding goal once you've initiated the campaign. You can always exceed the goal, which would be great. So set a modest goal that nonetheless will really help you start on your journey to self-sufficiency.

Promote Your Campaign

There are many different ways to make people aware of your crowdfunding campaign. Here are a few tips for getting the word out:

- ⟫ Use social media to spread the message.
- ⟫ Reach out to the media and bloggers to get coverage for your campaign.
- ⟫ Host a live event to drive up interest and engagement.

Keep in mind that your campaign is unlikely to succeed without a 100 percent commitment on your part. You need to think of it as a full-time job while you're driving toward your campaign goals. Leverage every relationship and marketing channel available to you.

Update Your Backers as Your Project Progresses

Keep your project backers in the loop as you move forward with your campaign. If you don't share regular updates with them, you could lose their interest, and you might not be able to attract as many pledgers as you would like.

Fortunately, crowdfunding platforms generally have built-in tools that allow you to update your project backers and send messages out to them. Take advantage of these tools and keep everyone in the loop.

Hype is unnecessary. Be honest and regular with your updates. If things aren't going exactly as you hoped they would, be transparent. Backers want to know that you can actually deliver on your project and the rewards you promised them.

Fulfill Your Promise

Your crowdfunding campaign isn't over if and when you reach your funding goals. It's over when you have fulfilled your promises. This means completing your project, delivering on your perks or rewards, and making sure you're communicating with your supporters every step of the way.

You can also use surveys to collect feedback from the pledgers at this stage, which will give you the information you need to improve your crowdfunding processes in the future.

Only when fulfillment is complete can you truly say you had a successful crowdfunding campaign. Until then, there are still a lot of things up in the air, both for you and for your backers.

Don't forget: Your backers are of primary importance. When you show them that you care, they'll be more willing to trust you and may even reach out to their friends to share your campaign with them.

Find a Viable Means to Monetize Your Pain Point

Fundamentally, the purpose of creating a new product is to solve a problem and alleviate a pain point. The pain point can be something mildly annoying or something that moves someone to change the world. For a crowdfunded product to be successful—and for any product to be successful—people must believe that it can alleviate one of their pain points.

"You need to be able to convey the value of the product if you want them to support your crowdfunding project. If they don't believe it will work, they won't back it. You might have created the solution to clean energy, but if people don't understand it or believe in it, you will never get the funding to make it happen," says Chalmers Brown, a serial entrepreneur and the cofounder of Due, an online invoicing platform.

While you can choose a project that solves a general pain point, tackling one of your own will help you easily forge an emotional connection with your backers. American Press, a coffee press that uses refillable pods, is a great example. Its creator, Alex Albanese, loved coffee but hated the mess, inefficiency, and environmental impact of existing brewing alternatives. His personal quest to create a quick, easy-to-clean, environmentally friendly way to brew coffee resulted in a product he was truly passionate about.

Find a Manufacturer You Can Work With

When you begin your campaign, your investors are going to want to know when they can expect to receive the product you've made them crave. The only way you can provide them with a reliable answer is to have a manufacturer ready to produce your designs.

Several factors can contribute to the length of time it will take to pick the perfect manufacturer. You need to decide if you want your product built locally or overseas and then find a company with business goals that mesh well with your own. Be sure you can easily communicate with your chosen manufacturing outfit.

According to Mass Fidelity, the phenomenally successful maker of The Core Wireless Speaker System, which raised $1.5 million on Indiegogo, one of the most important things you can do during a crowdfunding campaign is make sure you can deliver on shipping promises. This is only possible if you have a firm grasp of what the entire manufacturing process will entail from start to finish—and that begins with finding the right manufacturer.

Make Changes Based on Feedback

One of the most important things you can do before you try to crowdfund your product is to make sure you have taken the time to have people test and review it. The Luuup Litter Box was first introduced via infomercial in the 1990s, and it was a huge success. However, as with many television campaigns, it eventually lost traction and went out of production. The original backer for the litter box took that feedback and, with the help of her son, made improvements before launching their Kickstarter campaign.

Taking the time to examine what went right and what went wrong proved to be an excellent strategy for the Luuup inventor. The project's initial goal was a modest $35,114, but she raised nearly $1.2 million before the campaign ended. Then she and her son took their feedback lesson a step further to make their product even more awesome by adding a spill guard. The advice provided (and the extra money they raised) helped make the product more effective and in sync with what their customer base wanted.

Make sure you do the research, learn from others' experiences, and have a plan for everything. When you put in the work to ensure you can deliver your product, connect with users on an emotional level, solve one (or more) of their problems, and are willing to change and improve, you can succeed. Now you just need to get started.

It's no secret that crowdfunding campaigns can be a lot of work. With the right structure in place, you can meet and even exceed your funding goals, but don't expect it to come easily. If you don't succeed the first time, be willing to try again.

Use a Crowdfunding Marketing Company to Boost Your Reach

Krowdster is a leader among apps that helps you manage your crowdfunding campaign. You can use it to optimize your target audience, extend your social reach, and get in touch with journalists and media outlets to get more exposure for your campaign. The challenges of launching a successful crowdfunding campaign should be fairly apparent by now. Krowdster could prove to be an invaluable tool in meeting your funding goals. There are different pricing levels depending on the kind of marketing you're interested in, including Twitter marketing, access to a backer directory, media lists, and bundles of different services. Other crowdfunding marketing companies that help young businesses promote their crowdfunding campaigns include Funded Today and Agency 2.0.

Beating the Odds and Avoiding Failure

Although we've all heard of wildly successful crowdfunding campaigns, the truth is that most crowdfunding campaigns fail.

Their inability to get traction with backers wasn't necessarily because their products were unappealing. More often than not, the key reason a project fails to meet its goal is that the project owner underestimated the time and cost required to properly market that campaign.

The need for a marketing budget, then, is not just for reward-based campaigns; it applies to investment-based crowdfunding campaigns as well. You'll be using your planned marketing budget to pay for crowdfunding campaigns, whether they are rewards-based or investment-based. While top equity platforms promote the thousands of registered investors just waiting to discover the Next Big Thing on their sites, most of those platforms have criteria and costs for actually marketing a deal to those investors.

Just remember, there's a price tag for getting highlighted in that platform's weekly email or being promoted to its social media followers or featured in its webinars. To gain visibility, an entrepreneur must be ready to commit marketing dollars, or at the very least be willing to surrender (sometimes substantial) equity or warrants in their venture.

So how, exactly, do you maximize your marketing efforts? The section offers five tips.

Don't Launch without a Budget

While much can be done for free, like sharing your campaign via your social media channels, emailing your friends and family, and hosting offline meetups or launch parties, the most successful campaigns do incur costs. From shooting a video to buying online ads to launching a PR campaign and even hiring a graphic designer, many successful crowdfunding campaigns invest a minimum of $20,000 in marketing efforts. With thousands of active projects competing at any one time on many platforms, these campaigns need to invest in ways that help them look polished, stand out, and get noticed.

Ensure That Your Vendors Have Experience with Your Type of Campaign

Investing in a campaign manager or marketing expert doesn't always mean success. Take the case of Simon Thomson of social app Source. Despite extensively researching and interviewing PR and crowdfunding agencies to give his campaign the best possible chance, Thomson spent $20,000 with a well-known crowdfunding PR agency, only to be greatly disappointed in its work. "Quite quickly into the first three months of working with this agency," Thomson said, "we understood that the claims made about greatly increasing our social media presence on various platforms and having strong press relationships were false."

Thomson said he also discovered that the PR group was uncreative and unresponsive when faced with challenges or requests to help the campaign get back on track. In general, when selecting a PR or marketing firm, do your research. Look up some of their clients and campaigns and check out how they've fared. Almost all websites offer a way to contact the business. You've got nothing to lose reaching out to companies to see how satisfied they were with their choice of marketing or PR firm. You might even get tips for better alternatives. Be sure the PR group you're looking into is not only creative but can also support the specific type of campaign you are launching (sports, film, tech product, service, and so on).

Understand Who Does the Heavy Lifting

Many of the companies using crowdfunding today are actually organizations with their own substantial PR and marketing budgets—as well as a full back-office support staff of internal PR people, marketing experts, and financial backers fueling and helping their campaign.

Given this, you should clarify with any potential marketing vendor what it actually contributed to any campaigns it cites as examples of its past success. Review the vendor's press contacts and ask to interview previous clients to ensure that the success it's touting resulted from that vendor's own efforts rather than the work, staff, and budgets of the companies behind those successful campaigns.

Make Sure Your Copy Has the Appropriate Call to Action

Although you may successfully drive traffic to your campaign, what's key is to convert those viewers to backers. Thomson's app Source had 10,000 visits to its campaign page, yet it still had issues converting visitors to backers because its copy had not been drafted with the appropriate calls to action to encourage contributions. A *call to action* is a direct marketing appeal for the prospect to take some kind of action, whether that be buying, committing to something, or being willing to be reached for further contact.

Although Source's original campaign for $25,000 succeeded, the company had hoped to raise well beyond this sum and ended up launching a second campaign to meet its capital needs—this time, however, without the marketing budget it had previously lost on a nonperforming vendor.

Strive to Gain Early Momentum

One key to a successful crowdfunding campaign is to gain early momentum. Most platforms indicate that project owners should attract the first 30 percent of their support from their own networks before turning to PR. Then the first three days of any subsequent campaign are crucial.

At this juncture, founders should send a project-preview link to their inner circle in advance of their campaign launch and be diligent about keeping in contact, so these supporters will contribute as soon as the campaign goes live. Founders should also rely on PR—but not to drive backers the day they launch. Instead, the PR firm should be there to help entrepreneurs cross the chasm between the initial support they've had (from friends, family, and coworkers) and the supporters to whom they have no connection as yet.

If you're a founder contemplating crowdfunding, don't be misled by the handful of "hits" that seem to go viral and then easily amass thousands of supporters and funders. While any project can be successful, any attempt you make to raise significant funds will most likely need a well-planned and well-funded marketing and PR campaign.

Inside a Kickstarter Campaign: Reading Rainbow

When LeVar Burton and his team launched a Kickstarter campaign in the spring of 2014, the focus was simple: to raise enough money so that *Reading Rainbow*, the educational TV show loved by children of the 1980s and '90s, could be reborn for the digital generation.

The fundraising part turned out to be easy—the crowdfunding campaign blew past its initial $1 million goal, collecting a total of $5.4 million. What *Reading Rainbow*'s COO and president of digital publishing, Sangita Patel, didn't fully realize at the time was that the fundraising was simply the beginning of a long journey, one that would involve hundreds of emails, dozens of sleepless nights, and one exploding UPS truck.

The hard work began immediately after the crowdfunding campaign ended. *Reading Rainbow* had broken the record for the most individual backers on Kickstarter, raising money from more than 105,000 people. On the one hand, it was exhilarating and inspiring. At the same time, it was a lot of mini-investors to make happy.

"The caveat, or the cautionary tale, around that is—you can't satisfy 105,000 people," Patel says. "You know people are going to get a T-shirt that doesn't fit so they are going to want to return it. They are going to get a mug that broke and so they want another one, and so it is ongoing."

In exchange for donations, the *Reading Rainbow* campaign offered a wide variety of rewards, from tote bags and T-shirts to signed headshots and in-person school visits from Burton, *Reading Rainbow*'s host. Patel was in charge of making sure all these promises were fulfilled. The responsibility quickly took over her life. On top of the known challenges inherent in delivering each award to the correct backer, she had to contend with countless unpredictable detours—like when a UPS truck carrying 121 *Reading Rainbow* donor packages burst into flames after an accident that was, luckily, nonfatal.

"I have had a lot of sleepless nights," Patel says.

Managing the logistical challenges of fulfilling the rewards of the campaign was an unforeseen challenge, to be sure. The *Reading Rainbow* team was motivated by the tremendous outpouring of support from the public and an unwavering dedication to the cause of children's education.

The campaign itself was born out of Burton's desire to relaunch the *Reading Rainbow* iPad app he had created three years prior. He wanted to make the experience more interactive and accessible—not everyone has an iPad, after all—which eventually led to the crowdfunding campaign.

Skybrary, an interactive digital library with more than 500 titles, was the first *Reading Rainbow* product developed with money raised on Kickstarter. Available on the web, iPad, Kindle Fire, and Android, it builds on the original *Reading Rainbow* iPad app by adding a layer of interactive digital animation that helps kids connect with and understand what they're reading. New features include video field trips, audio guides, and memory games.

While the campaign raised millions more than its original goal, spending the entire $5.4 million was easy. A large chunk went to paying everyone involved in developing Skybrary, says Patel, and a significant percentage was spent fulfilling the rewards promised to the campaign's backers. Between 8 and 10 percent automatically went to Kickstarter and Amazon to cover service and credit card processing fees.

The remaining money was used to make Skybrary available to as many underserved classrooms as possible, says Teri Rousseau, president of educational services for *Reading Rainbow*. A one-year subscription to the *Reading Rainbow* Skybrary for a single classroom costs $179 for up to 35 students or $1,450 per school for up to 350 students. Schools have to apply, but with the money raised during the Kickstarter campaign, the *Reading Rainbow* Skybrary school program will be gifted to as many as 10,000 classrooms in need.

Over a summer, *Reading Rainbow* beta tested Skybrary in 30 classrooms. The team received thank-you cards from grateful students. These notes became Patel's anchor; whenever she encountered a new logistical problem or received yet another email from a dissatisfied campaign backer, she found strength in the knowledge that she was making a difference in kids' lives.

"That was the only thing that kept me going," she says.

Helping Startups Stand Out: Q&A with SeedInvest's Ryan Feit

Ryan Feit and James Han wanted their crowdfunding site to be more than a listing service for startups in search of cash. So, when the former investors launched New York City–based SeedInvest in 2012, they handpicked the companies they wanted to include. The idea was to make it easier for startups to stand out from the crowd and give accredited investors the highest caliber of companies from which to choose.

As of 2023, more than 300,000 investors had signed on and more than 250 companies have been funded, with total funding raised surpassing $200 million. In addition to companies actively fundraising, SeedInvest features "prospects"—select up-and-comers showcased to gauge investor interest.

Once cleared to begin fundraising, startups must specify a target amount and deadline; to collect the funds, they must meet both. SeedInvest takes a 5 percent equity fee and charges a 7.5 percent placement fee from funds raised through the site. In 2016, *Entrepreneur* talked to Feit about SeedInvest's curated approach:

Entrepreneur: *What qualities do you look for in startups?*

Feit: We definitely evaluate the team to see if their experience fits the market they're going after. We'll also look at whether it's a large enough market for investors. We'll look at the competitive landscape and figure out if they have something that differentiates them from other people. We'll look at funding traction as well. Although it's not a requirement, a lot of the deals that have done well on our site are deals where an angel group or a VC or maybe some other investors have already committed to the company.

Entrepreneur: *What must companies submit to be considered?*

Feit: We require them to submit an investor deck, which should have walked through a lot of the things that I mentioned we're looking for. Then we want to see a little historical [info] if they have that, and projections. From that we can typically tell whether they're ready or whether they need more work.

Entrepreneur: *How long does it take to get funded?*

Feit: Based on what we're seeing, it should take between a week and a few months. But it really depends on the company, how much they're trying to raise, and their investor traction.

Entrepreneur: *What are your repayment terms?*

Feit: We don't have a standardized template. It's ultimately a negotiation between the entrepreneur and the investor, and typically the terms are not any different than they would be from raising capital offline.

Entrepreneur: *What are some of the site's unique features?*

Feit: We have something called Virtual Meetings. It allows an entrepreneur to pitch investors across the country from their couch. The second feature we've built is called Simple Invest. That allows investors to sign legal documents and send money to fund their investment in a few easy steps. As an entrepreneur, you never have to track down a check or a signature page again. And we're building a feature called Groups, which allows VCs, angel groups, incubators, and other affinity groups to have their own portion of SeedInvest. As we bring on more investment groups, it will help entrepreneurs on our site access them.

Entrepreneur: *Any advice for entrepreneurs interested in SeedInvest?*

Feit: It's really important to get as far as you can as an entrepreneur prior to raising capital. Spend some time and a little bit of money to make sure you have a product that is ready to launch. Speak with as many investors as you can before the SeedInvest process. It helps your cause if you have some investors that are interested when you launch your deal on our site.

The Top 10 Crowdfunding Platforms

Several parameters were used to come up with the top 10 crowdfunding platforms. These parameters include the platform's popularity, reviews, charges, ease of use, and more. Following are the top 10 crowdfunding platforms:

10. Experiment

Founded in 2012, this New York City–based platform helps to discover, fund, and share scientific research. You can register a project for free on this platform, but once you get all the funds, Experiment charges an 8 percent platform fee. Its payment processing fee is between 3 to 5 percent. So far, it has funded almost 1,000 projects.

9. CircleUp

Founded in 2012, this San Francisco–based company assists early-stage consumer brands with capital and resources. Moreover, it offers both equity capital and credit financing. This crowdfunding platform is backed by Canaan Partners, Collaborative Fund, QED Advisors, Union Square Ventures, GV, as well as former leaders of Goldman Sachs, Capital One, and Stanford Endowment. The platform determines charges on a case-by-case basis.

8. LendingClub

Founded in 2006, this San Francisco–based company offers up to $40,000 in personal loans and up to $300,000 in business loans. Unlike some other equity crowdfunding, this company doesn't require things such as business visits or plans and projects. A company interested in getting a loan from LendingClub should be in business for at least one year, have annual sales of $50,000, no recent bankruptcies, and ownership of at least 20 percent of the business.

7. SeedInvest Technology

Founded in 2012, this New York–based crowdfunding platform is regarded as the best way for early-stage startups to raise funds. Since its inception, the platform has attracted more than 300,000 investors. It has helped more than 200 startups to raise over $200 million in funds. SeedInvest has a 7.5 percent placement fee on the amount raised through the platform, as well as a 5 percent equity fee.

6. GoFundMe

Founded in 2010, this crowdfunding platform helps people raise funds for almost everything from personal health-care expenses to keeping local businesses alive. It is not an all-or-nothing fundraising site, meaning users keep the funds they raise. GoFundMe collects a 2.9 percent processing fee and 30 cents for every donation. Some of its successful campaigns include $11.8 million for the Las Vegas Victims Fund and $24.2 million for the Time's Up Legal Defense Fund.

5. Patreon

Founded in 2013, this crowdfunding site was the idea of YouTube musician Jack Conte. As can be expected, this platform is popular among digital creatives, such as bloggers, YouTubers, and podcasters. Unlike other platforms that collect one-off campaign donations, this platform has a subscription model. The users (patrons) need to regularly donate a set amount every month or per creation. It charges a fee of 2.9 percent and 30 cents from each pledge.

4. Crowdfunder

Founded in 2012, this Los Angeles–based company is an equity crowdfunding platform that helps to fund high-growth ventures. It has a network of more than 130,000 entrepreneurs and investors. The company claims to have a community of 12,000 individual and institutional investors. So far, this crowdfunding platform has funded about 60 deals with an average deal size of $1.8 million. Crowdfunder offers three pricing plans: Free, Starter ($299/month), and Premium ($499/month).

3. Crowd Supply

Founded in 2012, this Portland-based platform claims to be the launchpad for "hardware, hackables and high-end goods." It was founded by a team of product engineers from MIT Media Lab. Some of the notable product launches on the platform are the Novena laptop by bunnie & xobs, Circuit Stickers by Chibitronics, and Purism's Librem laptop. In terms of pricing, Crowd Supply offers many plans, including a Standard plan with 5 percent of gross campaign sales.

2. Indiegogo

Founded in 2008, this crowdfunding platform has helped to fund over 800,000 ideas since its inception. The platform gets about 10 million visitors a month and about 19,000 campaigns list on Indiegogo on a monthly basis. Indiegogo allows users to promote their campaign on other platforms, such as Facebook and Google. Its charges are a 5 percent platform fee and a third-party processing fee of 3 to 5 percent.

1. Kickstarter

Founded in 2009, this crowdfunding platform helps tech and creative entrepreneurs to fund their projects initially. As of January 2021, the company has raised more than $5.6 billion with over 197,425 projects. Those interested in raising money through this platform need to set up their goal along with a time period to complete it. It is an all-or-nothing platform, meaning you need to meet the set goal within the allotted time, or else the money goes back. Kickstarter charges a 5 percent fee in addition to the processing payment charges.

Playing by the SEC's New Rules: Understanding the JOBS Act

This section talks about what you need to know about the Securities and Exchange Commission (SEC)'s equity crowdfunding rules and how to comply. This dictates how you market your campaign and otherwise reach out to nonaccredited and accredited equity investors about your fundraising campaign.

Title III and Regulation A+

Under Title III of the JOBS Act, small businesses can use an online crowdfunding portal to sell equity in their business to the general public and to raise up to $1 million in capital. Equity crowdfunding under the JOBS Act has been seen as a democratization of the startup and small business investment process, and one that puts the ability of entrepreneurs to raise capital into the hands of "the crowd" and not just wealthy investors, banks, and Wall Street brokers.

Title IV, or "Regulation A+," holds even more excitement for some, given that it allows a small or emerging business to raise up to $50 million in capital from "the crowd" through a relatively inexpensive form of public offering.

Until now, donation-based and rewards-based crowdfunding (offering products and merchandise in return for donations) have been the two most popular vehicles for entrepreneurs using this concept to fund their startups and other projects. But now Regulation A+ is the new kid on the funding block. Regulation A+ could potentially change the landscape in the long run by easing restrictions on equity-based crowdfunding. A+ is categorized by two tiers:

1. Tier 1 is for smaller offerings raising up to $20 million in any 12-month period.
2. Tier 2 is for offerings raising up to $50 million in the same time period.

Regulation A+ is meant to entice more midsize and larger businesses to try crowdfunding, as it essentially allows businesses to go public without launching an actual IPO.

Regulation A+ "ups the ante" in several ways for entrepreneurs in the crowdfunding arena. First, businesses participating in equity crowdfunding must be incorporated and meet extensive compliance and reporting requirements due to the complex nature of the business arrangement (i.e., bringing investors into your company).

Second, A+ changes public solicitation for equity crowdfunding by loosening restrictions on the use of the web and social media for these offerings. As a result, the crowdfunding market is likely to become noisier than ever.

When it comes to equity-based crowdfunding, there are still many unanswered questions: What will be allowed under the law, for example, and what not-so-obvious liabilities are out there? Any business considering equity crowdfunding—or, indeed, any other form of crowdfunding—should build and maintain relationships with its trusted advisors, such as lawyers and accountants.

Women Raise More Money with Crowdfunding

Women raise more money with crowdfunding than men do because of the words female founders tend to use, according to one study.

Women generally use words that talk about positive emotions—for example, "excited" and "happy"—and inclusivity, such as preferring the pronoun "we" and words such as "together." That kind of language is associated with crowdfunding campaigns that, all other factors being relatively equal, raise more money, says UC Berkeley Haas School of Business assistant professor Andreea Gorbatai.

"Using inclusive language builds this bond of trust, where you feel that people are not trying to take your money—you feel that they are including you in this venture," Gorbatai says.

For her research, Gorbatai examined 9,943 campaigns on the San Francisco–based crowdfunding platform Indiegogo. Approximately two-thirds of the campaigns studied were small business related, and the remaining third were technology related. All were spearheaded by one entrepreneur, as opposed to a founding team.

To isolate the effect that language has on the amount of money a crowdfunding campaign raises, Gorbatai used an "exact matching technique," with which she studied two campaigns that were raising the same amount of money for a similar reason over a similar period of time, where the only difference was that one was run by a female founder and the other was run by a male founder. For the purposes of the study, a campaign was considered a success over another if it raised more money.

That those fundraising campaigns organized by women tend to raise more money than those run by men runs counter to most other fundraising gender dynamics. "Online fundraising settings pose an interesting empirical puzzle: Women are systematically more successful than men, an outcome contrary to offline gender inequality," she writes. For example, venture capital funds tend to be overwhelmingly distributed by men to other men, Gorbatai points out in her paper.

To be sure, crowdfunding investors have different motivations than traditional investors. While traditional investors are overwhelmingly putting their money behind projects that are expected to see positive financial return, crowdfunding investors "give money in order to support projects they value for social or value-related reasons," Gorbatai writes. That's one reason why language plays such a pivotal role. Those seeking crowdfunding dollars need to convince potential investors of the moral and sociological worth of their cause. And they must do so often without the benefit of face-to-face time spent building relationships.

Streamlining the Investor Roadshow: FlashFunders

In late 2014, Eric Wolfe scored $1.2 million in equity capital for Swapt, the apartment rental platform he debuted earlier in the year. Despite raising money from investors in the U.S., Europe, and Australia, he didn't have to fly to dozens of pitch meetings. Nor did he have to pay tens of thousands of dollars in legal overhead to close the round. Instead, the San Francisco entrepreneur used FlashFunders, a no-fee online equity investment platform that launched in 2014. "It streamlined the process," Wolfe says.

That's the idea, says Vincent Bradley, FlashFunders cofounder and CEO. He points out that raising seed capital can take six months and costs startups an average of $23,000 in legal fees alone. "That is a material amount of time and money that should be spent building your business," Bradley explains. "FlashFunders is reinventing the investor roadshow."

The Santa Monica–based platform provides entrepreneurs with SEC-compliant investment documents and access to FDIC-insured escrow accounts, which it helps manage.

"If you're a startup trying to raise capital, and one of your venture firms finds out that you've done it in a noncompliant manner, you've basically made yourself toxic for future financing rounds," Bradley says.

If you want in on the action, here's what you need to know.

How It Works

Startups listed on FlashFunders set their own valuation, determine how much money to raise, and decide on the duration of the campaign (Bradley suggests capping it at 30 to 60 days). Campaigns are an all-or-nothing affair; startups must raise the entire amount or walk away with nothing.

The default minimum investment is $2,500 per party, though founders can increase this amount if they choose. (Swapt, for example, set a minimum of $10,000 per investor.) If a campaign exceeds its minimum funding goal, the startup can continue to accept investments up to a predetermined maximum amount. Once funded, startups work with a FlashFunders advisor to issue stock certificates to investors and file necessary federal and state securities paperwork.

FlashFunders campaigns have sought up to $500,000, Bradley says. But the site welcomes brick-and-mortar businesses looking for less capital (think a friendly neighborhood café in search of $50,000).

What It (Really) Costs

FlashFunders' fee-free status for investors and entrepreneurs is here to stay. "We don't want to nickel-and-dime people," Bradley says. Instead, the platform reserves the right to buy an additional 25 percent of securities from startups that meet their fundraising goals for up to three years, at the same price and terms granted other investors. After FlashFunders' initial investment in that startup, the platform may invest in any future offerings the company makes.

How to Use It

To raise money on FlashFunders, startups must fill out a questionnaire and submit to background checks. FlashFunders also reviews applicants' business plans to help viable companies fine-tune what Bradley calls their "investment thesis."

Including a video and clearly outlining how you'll spend the money raised helps make your case. "You have to provide enough material so investors can make an informed decision," Bradley advises. "Be prepared. Know what your idea is. And sell yourself. Angel investors are looking for great people to invest in."

Three Lessons from the Top 50 Rewards-Based Crowdfunding Campaigns

An analysis of the top 50 highest-funded, rewards-based crowdfunding campaigns reveals that the most successful campaigns aren't launched impulsively but are well thought out and organized. Here are three considerations for business owners interested in launching successful crowdfunding campaigns.

Incorporate Your Business

Incorporation reduces your personal liabilities; enables you to take advantage of certain loans, grants, and contracts; and helps you stay in compliance with the law. Nine out of ten of the most successful rewards-based crowdfunding campaigns were launched by incorporated businesses.

Create a Video about Your Business and Campaign

Videos help tell your story and are an important element of the social media landscape. One hundred percent of the most successful rewards-based crowdfunding campaigns had them.

Build a Large Social Media Following

The average social media following for rewards-based crowdfunding campaigns—across the six platforms studied—was 310,202. One campaign had as many as 9.7 million followers, due in large part to its extensive presence on YouTube.

CHAPTER 8

Scouting the Alternative Lending Landscape

One Google search can turn up dozens of "alternative lenders" and newfangled lending platforms. *Alternative lending* refers to lending that takes place outside of traditional financial institutions. Compared to going through a traditional process, alternative lending happens online and is typically faster and easier to acquire. This chapter aims to help you navigate these alternatives by walking through some of the most prevalent types of online and alternative lenders and giving readers the skinny on each. The main message here is to keep your eyes wide open and pay attention to details. Some costs may be larger than they initially sound and some terms more onerous.

Why Small Businesses Are Turning to Online Lenders

Small business owners can have a particularly difficult time getting capital from a bank if they have been in business fewer than two years or if their credit score is low. Fortunately, there are alternatives to the traditional bank installment loan. Online lending has been a source of innovation and promise for small businesses that are looking to invest and grow. Just be aware that this type of loan typically costs more than a traditional loan—roughly double, according to one study. And there are standards. Alternative loans are not always easy to get.

There are many forms of alternate finance, from peer-to-peer platforms to ones that are more akin to institutional lenders, but with much more flexibility. The lending formats are very diverse as well, ranging from mortgages and payday loans to loans disbursed in cryptocurrency. For entrepreneurs and investors, alternate lending is a gold mine that's changing the rules of finance and opening up new opportunities.

Profitable Investments

The evolution of alternative lending has moved from the days when it was mostly dominated by peer-to-peer platforms with some institutional underwriting to a present landscape where it's largely run by companies building their proprietary platforms to make the process as effective and scalable as possible while maximizing profitability.

Many hedge funds now participate actively in the alternative lending market, showing that the industry is rapidly becoming a major competitor to traditional finance models. It's particularly enticing for investors who are looking for higher returns and are willing to handle higher risk.

According to Daniel Wessels, CEO of Jacaranda Finance, "They'll be able to benefit from the attractive yield and short duration, which means there'll be some insulation from rising benchmark interest rates." Alternative loan arrangements like amortization are also more flexible, as opposed to most traditional loans whose principal is paid back on maturity.

Big Data

Big data is a major driver of all sectors of the fintech revolution, and alternative lending is no exception. Many companies now operating in this space have begun to deviate from the traditional systems of rating an applicant's creditworthiness as determined by the major national credit bureaus.

Now, with the ability to collect and process data at an unprecedented scale, lenders can evaluate thousands of data points. The effects of this approach are that alternative lenders are able to capture segments of the population that would have been rated poorly in traditional metrics, not necessarily because they aren't creditworthy, but because their lifestyles do not fit into the normal metrics. An example is some millennials who don't use credit cards and other groups that don't actively use the traditional banking system.

Some alternative lending companies now use information from unconventional (and, frankly, sometimes weird) sources to evaluate applicants, such as how they shop, the activities they use their phones for (including the games they play), and even how well they organize their contact lists. Although there are legitimate concerns regarding privacy and data security, what's clear is that big data is revolutionizing finance, and alternative lending is the frontier of that revolution.

Enabling Diverse Industries

There have traditionally been industries deemed more appropriate to invest in, especially for institutional lenders. Those perspectives haven't changed as fast as the realities in society and the financial industry have, leaving some industries with high profitability stranded in terms of being able to access financing.

The legal cannabis business, for instance, still struggles to find funding from traditional banks (primarily as a result of the fact that, technically, cannabis cultivation, processing, and sale is still illegal federally). This situation has made it possible for investors to provide funds to promising cannabusinesses, benefiting from the high patronage and profits while also balancing the risks of a rapidly evolving regulatory landscape.

Over time, more industries like that will begin to emerge, and the flexibility of alternative lending will be a major positive factor in how quickly and effectively entrepreneurs and investors can reach agreements that enable innovation and business expansion while making profits for all parties involved.

The Upside of Alternative Lending

Small business owners are turning to online lenders because the new creditors offer loan products that better fit their financing needs. These days, many small business owners do not need term loans to make major purchases, but instead require relatively small amounts of money to manage short-term cash flow emergencies.

Online lenders are well-positioned to meet this demand. Their loans tend to be smaller in magnitude and shorter in duration than traditional bank loans, a report by consultancy group Oliver Wyman found. Many online lenders also offer cash advances against accounts receivable, a type of financing that is especially helpful in smoothing out lumpy cash flow.

Small business owners are also attracted by the simple, rapid application processes with web-based lenders. In a survey of its customers, online lender OnDeck Capital found a significant number of them rejected the idea of borrowing from traditional credit sources because getting a loan from these lenders is "too difficult" and "takes too long."

Online lenders have accelerated and simplified the loan-application, decision, and funds-disbursal processes. Estimates show that applications at these creditors take as little as 2 percent of the time to complete as those at traditional banks. Moreover, online lenders tend to accept or reject financing requests in hours, rather than the weeks it takes at banks.

Most small business owners believe that time, not money, is their most precious resource. They favor credit products that save them time, even if they cost more. Online lending is growing because many small business owners are willing to pay higher interest rates to quickly and painlessly obtain loans that precisely match their funding needs.

Navigating Online Lending Options

How can small business owners save time and get the most value out of the online lending process? This section discusses key tips and insights for applying for a small business loan online.

> *Ensure your finances are in order.* Online lending provides more adaptability and flexibility than traditional banks, but you should still provide solid business records confirming your company is viable and can repay the money you borrow. Start with the basics: Make sure you have a registered business name and have incorporated your business with a tax ID number and a business checking account.

> *Use online accounting software.* Digital tools like QuickBooks, FreshBooks, Kashoo, or Xero can help even the smallest business manage their finances with accuracy and efficiency. Zoho Books is another option, and it's even free. With your information available digitally, it's easier to track your finances and prove you're a desirable loan candidate. Some services, such as NetSuite, provide advanced automation, regulatory, and cloud tools.

> *Keep business finances separate from personal finances.* Your business should have a financial identity separate from your personal finances. If you pay invoices with personal checks or credit cards, you run the risk of overcomplicating your finances or not passing an audit. Establish a separate bank account and credit card to manage all your business spending under your business name.

> *Understand fees (especially hidden fees) from online lenders.* Pay attention to the fine print of any loan application. Ask questions up front to ensure you understand loan fees, interest, originations, and any other costs you'll pay for your loan.

> *Research the qualities of each lender, such as customer service, price, and more.* Other than access to capital, what do you need most from your small business lender? Compare your options and read customer reviews on sites like Trustpilot (www.trustpilot.com). The lowest-priced loan option might not always be the best fit, especially

if other small business owners report hidden fees or hassles with customer service.

▷ *Keep an eye on security.* Getting a loan online might seem riskier than going through a traditional bank, but a few basic precautions can help you keep your personal information safe. First, research each lender to make sure the company is reputable. Second, confirm you're sending any financial information via a secure website connection. That means the URL starts with https://. Finally, be wary of any lender that asks for an up-front application fee or an immediate down payment before your loan is approved. Legitimate lenders will package any fees as part of the overall repayment plan rather than charging you up front.

There has never been a better time to get small business financing online. Using these tips can help you weigh your options to get the funding you need to grow your business.

No Credit? No Problem: OnDeck

One loan product gives businesses access to up to a quarter million dollars in cash in 24 hours. But make no mistake: It is going to cost you.

Small business lending company OnDeck Capital offers term loans that can provide small business owners up to $250,000 in as little as 24 hours with up to 24 months to repay the balance. OnDeck is a technology-based lender that uses data, like a business owner's cash flow, to determine whether to disburse a loan. The company also offers a different product, an ongoing line of credit up to $100,000.

The loan offering is not for startups. OnDeck is for business owners looking to expand into another store location, purchase a very large piece of equipment, or make some other significant business investment.

To apply for the OnDeck loan, a company must have been in business for at least one year with gross monthly income of at least $100,000 and have stable business checking account balances. Also, at least one of the owners must have a personal credit score of 625 or higher.

In exchange for such speed and convenience, you pay, of course. The annual percentage rates may vary, so check www.ondeck.com for current rates. OnDeck automatically deducts a payment from the business owner's checking account daily or weekly over the life of the loan to recoup the debt.

OnDeck is very transparent about the cost of the loan. It breaks down—clearly, not in that infamous "fine print"—exactly how much a loan from them is going to cost. Its sweet spot, though, is serving business owners who have an opportunity that would require cash up front and can't wait for a bank loan. While bank loans have lower interest rates, they also take a lot longer to secure.

At the time of writing, TrustPilot rates OnDeck 4.6 out of 5 stars.

One other option you might consider, if you happen to have valuable personal assets such as expensive jewelry or watches, is an online "pawnshop" such as Borro. Read the terms very carefully if you try this route.

Matching Small Businesses with Creditors: Q&A with Olya Losina

When the economy tanked in 2008, enrollment in Olya Losina's fledgling art school began to wane. Marketing the San Diego–based Losina Art Center to a new crop of students required cash the painter and her husband / business partner, Bill Beatty, didn't have. So, in late 2011, they created a profile on Lendio (www.lendio.com), a free online service that matches small businesses with lenders. Within minutes, they had a customized list of half a dozen potential lenders offering the five-figure, short-term financing they were seeking, and within days, they received the cash they needed.

In a conversation with *Entrepreneur*, Losina sketched out how Lendio and her specific lender, OnDeck, helped keep her art school afloat:

Entrepreneur: Why did you go online for your cash infusion?

Losina: When the economy took a hit, our students pulled back. All of a sudden they just couldn't spend any money, and it left us struggling. We couldn't get ahead enough to do any marketing to expand. We needed to take out a small loan to build the business. The banks didn't want to talk to us; we'd destroyed our personal credit opening the business. We're renting our place, so we don't have equity. What interested us about Lendio is that they didn't look at equity; they looked at the cash flow. And we could show that.

Entrepreneur: *What was it like working with Lendio?*

Losina: It was a simple process. We filled out a quick questionnaire, and Lendio got us in touch with qualified lenders without us having to research and qualify them ourselves. This definitely helped save us time. We scheduled a follow-up conversation with our Lendio representative, who gave us tips on how to evaluate lenders. Then we spoke to a few of them. And we took time making sure OnDeck was legitimate.

Entrepreneur: *What did OnDeck ask of you?*

Losina: They weren't looking at our personal credit score; they were looking at our cash flow and whether we'd be able to pay the loan back. The time from when we submitted our loan documents to OnDeck to the time the money showed up in our account was three to four days.

Entrepreneur: *What were your loan repayment terms?*

Losina: We qualified for $15,000, but we took only $10,000. It was an 86-day loan, paid back on a daily basis. The amount we were paying back was just $127 a day. We were getting a couple of new students a week, so it was a number we could deal with. But coming up with an extra $3,000 a month all in one chunk—it would have been paralyzing to see a big number like that. The loan ended up costing 10 percent to pay back over those months. It was not a hard decision to make. We used that $10,000 to make more money.

Entrepreneur: *How did you spend the cash?*

Losina: We used the money for brochures, a major upgrade to our website, and creating videos for the site. We started a program to help students create and put together a winning portfolio to get into art college. We created a video with one of our students who got into a very competitive college. He came to us with no drawing skills whatsoever. We saw that there was a real market for the portfolio program, so we're continuing to push it as a standalone product. The money we got helped us create that program; now it's 10 percent of our business.

More Brilliant Financial and Capital Ideas

Here are some more people and companies involved in alternative lending. The variety of thinking in this space is constantly evolving:

- ≫ The Harvard Business School grads behind the WomenVCFundII invest in businesses with at least one woman in a leadership role because they believe gender-diverse teams make better decisions, higher-quality products, and, ultimately, higher profits.
- ≫ Zest AI improves on traditional underwriting models by using machine learning and large-scale data analysis to make credit available to more people without raising the risk to lenders.
- ≫ The FlashFunders equity investment platform streamlines the fundraising process by offering entrepreneurs SEC-compliant documents and FDIC-insured escrow accounts, saving them thousands in legal fees.
- ≫ Online financial service Fundbox offers working capital and spend management solutions to help small businesses optimize cash flow.
- ≫ Most angel investors are men. To get more female financiers onto term sheets, Pipeline Angels offers boot camps in 30-plus U.S. cities that teach women the fine art of angel investing.
- ≫ London-based Earthport aimed to upend the archaic process by which money is sent overseas. Acquired by Visa and rolled into its Visa Direct service in 2019, Earthport's centralized, cloud-based network technology has significantly simplified the transfer of money around the world.
- ≫ The Aspiration platform for middle-class investors has a "pay what is fair" approach to fees and donates 10 percent of revenue to charitable causes.

As you can see just from this small sampling, the variety and creativity out there in the alternative lending landscape knows no bounds. Do your homework, get online, talk to friends, family, and colleagues, and you're sure to scare up even more examples of new concepts in lending.

Royalty Financing: Financing without Taking On Debt or Giving Away Equity

Serial entrepreneur Aamer Sarfraz knows that raising money to launch or grow your business is painful, and says he has invented a better way.

Sarfraz aims to bring royalty financing to entrepreneurs. Instead of compensating investors with equity, entrepreneurs raising an R round through Sarfraz's firm Draper Oakwood Royalty Capital will pay investors back with a small percentage of their future earnings.

The investment house had something of a soft launch in January 2016, though it hadn't yet made any investments, as it was waiting for the U.K. federal regulatory paperwork to be approved.

401(k)—A Possible Last Resort: Turning Your Retirement into Financing for Your Business with ROBS

Note: The method of funding a business described in this section should be considered only in close partnership with a financial planner or accountant who has done it before. There are too many ways for you to run afoul of the IRS, and the consequences can include the loss of your retirement funds. And *only* consider it if you have a big retirement account *and* bad credit, because it is a way to tap financing that is not a loan, so there is no loan application process and there are no loan payments.

How It Works

A Rollover as Business Startup (with the all-too-apt acronym ROBS) is a scheme whereby you turn your retirement into financing for your business, which you create as a C Corporation. As the IRS puts it, "The ROBS plan then uses the rollover assets to purchase the stock of the new C Corporation business."

While not illegal as a concept, the IRS tends to pay special attention to ROBS cases and has several methods at its disposal to trip them up or stop them. Threading the ROBS needle is therefore complicated and fraught with financial and even legal peril.

Typically, the way to do it is to work with an outside company that promotes the idea and promises to guide you through the process (see next section for details). According to the IRS:

"Promoters aggressively market ROBS arrangements to prospective business owners. In many cases, the company will apply to IRS for a favorable determination letter (DL) as a way to assure their clients that IRS approves the ROBS arrangement. The IRS issues a DL based on the plan's terms meeting Internal Revenue Code (Code) requirements. DLs do not give plan sponsors protection from incorrectly applying the plan's terms or from operating the plan in a discriminatory manner. When a plan sponsor administers a plan in a way that results in prohibited discrimination or engages in prohibited transactions, the plan can be disqualified, which can result in adverse tax consequences to the plan's sponsor and its participants."

The IRS conducted research into ROBS and found the following:

▷ Most ROBS plans failed (to be fair, so do most businesses in general)
▷ High rates of bankruptcy in the aftermath
▷ Large recurring promoter fees and legal issues
▷ Running afoul of the required filing of Form 5500, Form 1120, or Form 1099-R
▷ Violations of legal codes after the fact because of changes to the plan

Bottom line: Work closely with a financial professional who has experience in ROBS rollovers. Do not attempt it on your own, given the numerous pitfalls and dire consequences of losing your retirement savings. All that said, it has been done, as you'll see in the next section.

Working with ROBS-Promoting Companies

One of the early adopters of this strategy, Gary Cote, used $60,000 from his 401(k) back in 2005 to start Sunray Technology Ventures, a California provider of high-speed internet access services for hotels (sadly, Mr. Cote passed away in 2012). "I didn't want to borrow money or mortgage our home to the hilt," Cote said. "Using my retirement money gave me independence. We've been profitable since 2007. I can't say enough about the scenario that allowed us to provide for all these people."

Although the mechanism for rolling retirement funds into business startups has been available for decades, the practice began in earnest in 2000, when industry founders and former business associates Leonard Fischer, founder and chairman of the board of Benetrends Financial of North Wales, Pennsylvania, and Steven Cooper, president of SDCooper of Huntington Beach, California, introduced the concept at the annual convention of the International Franchise Association. "We were the hit of the show," Cooper says. Rollovers gained momentum during the early 2000s but fell out of favor during the boom years before the Great Recession, when credit was easily available.

Be aware that retirement rollovers are not as simple as they may sound. Obviously, you are putting your nest egg in jeopardy. Less obviously, you also usually agree to pay a rollover plan provider an annual fee for the life of your business and, some tax experts warn, risk increased scrutiny from the IRS. As mentioned in the previous section, the IRS studies such plans and regards them with what might be called skepticism or pessimism.

The "long-standing provision" behind these plans is ERISA, the extremely complicated and easy-to-violate Employee Retirement Income Security Act of 1974, which enables employees to be responsible for their own retirement plans.

The three main administrators of rollover plans—SDCooper, Benetrends, and Guidant Financial—have tweaked ERISA rules into a neat three-step program. You pay them a fee, which is not small and can vary, and it'll do the rest: Move your current 401(k) or IRA (self-directed IRAs are not eligible) into an ERISA profit-sharing plan, which then becomes the retirement plan for your new company. That plan buys up the stock of your new C corporation. Once the funds have transferred, they become tax-free capital for your business. In essence, you are spending the money on your own corporation instead of on stock in another company, such as General Electric or Goldman Sachs.

"You then open a corporate checking account," Cooper says, "and pay yourself back for whatever you've spent money on and pay our fees." Like the other providers, Cooper charges an annual fee to file documents required by the IRS to make sure your new "retirement plan" remains safely qualified.

Compliance is easy when starting out, when you are the only employee and the stock value is low. In a Benetrends survey, almost three-fourths of clients had only one to three employees. Of the rest, 14 percent employed seven or more, and 3 percent had 21 or more workers. Half of all clients' employees participated or planned to participate in their employers' retirement plans, and the IRS wants to make sure those plans are viable.

How did Gary Cote end up? Cote's rollover started both a business and a rich new retirement plan. He opened his Sunray retirement plan to his employees and moved some of its funds into stocks and bonds. He hired professional appraisers to evaluate the assets in his plan, and every year his provider, Guidant, helped him file detailed reports with the IRS. "My own retirement plan," Cote said, "is worth substantially more than the $60,000 that was in it five years ago."

CHAPTER 9

Wooing Angels and Venture Capitalists

A ngel investors and venture capital (VC) firms are often regarded as the holy grail of startup financiers. This chapter pulls back the covers on how to approach them, when to approach them, what to expect, and what makes a good deal. It also examines what VCs are looking for in terms of the Next Big Thing, and how to assemble your investor dream team.

You should start your list of targets at least a year before you'll need the money and start networking right now. The chapter also covers getting those coveted warm introductions via LinkedIn and through your contact network. Let's start by defining some terms.

Originally a term used to describe investors in Broadway shows, *angel* now refers to anyone who invests his or her money in an entrepreneurial company (unlike institutional venture capitalists, who invest other people's money). Angel investing has soared in recent years as a growing number of individuals seek better returns on their money than they can get from traditional investment vehicles. Contrary to popular belief, most angels are not millionaires. Typically, they earn between $60,000 and $100,000 a year. Which means there are likely to be plenty of them right in your own backyard.

Angels come in two varieties: those you know and those you don't know. They may include professionals such as doctors and lawyers; business associates such as executives, suppliers, and customers; and even other entrepreneurs. Unlike venture capitalists and bankers, many angels are not motivated solely by profit. Particularly if your angel is a current or former entrepreneur, they may be motivated as much by the enjoyment of helping a young business succeed as by the money they stand to gain. Angels are more likely than venture capitalists to be persuaded by an entrepreneur's drive to succeed, persistence, and mental discipline.

Venture capital refers to funds flowing into a company, generally during pre-IPO process, in the form of an investment rather than a loan. Controlled by an individual or small group known as *venture capitalists* (VCs), these investments require a high rate of return and are secured by a substantial ownership position in the business.

VCs represent the most glamorous and appealing form of financing to many entrepreneurs. They're known for backing high-growth companies in the early stages, and many of the best-known entrepreneurial success stories owe their growth to financing from venture capitalists. VCs can provide large sums of money, advice, and prestige by their mere presence. Just the fact that you've obtained venture capital backing means your business has, in venture capitalists' eyes, at least, considerable potential for rapid and profitable growth.

Seed funding, as its name suggests, just means early funding—the first influx of cash meant to help a business get off the ground and start running. Seed funding can come from a variety of sources, including venture capital, outside investors, friends and family, or even yourself. Series A funding refers to the first big round of venture capital funding. In particular, it is the name given to the preferred class of stock purchased by the VC in exchange for the funding. Series A funding is often significant and is meant to fund a company for the short-to-medium term, from approximately six months to a year or two. Subsequent rounds of funding are given similar names, such as Series B, Series C, and so forth.

A word of caution: Some entrepreneurs pay fees to pitch at angel events or to just rub elbows with accredited investors. No reputable company should charge for this type of thing. Hardworking business owners may give away large percentages of their ventures because they are raising capital too early, when it is more difficult to assess the value of their companies. Some entrepreneurs have the mistaken impression that as long as they have a good idea, a venture capitalist will write them a check, with no groundwork having been laid. Their focus is merely this: "If only I could meet some investors, I could launch my company."

Anatomy of a VC Deal: How One Seattle Startup Raised $12.5 Million

Kristen Hamilton knew she needed to raise capital to get her Seattle-based startup off the ground. She and cofounder Josh Jarrett spent half of 2013 developing Koru, an immersive business program that gives recent college graduates real-world job skills and positions them for rewarding entry-level work.

That fall, the pair enlisted a handful of Whitman College graduates to participate in a weeklong pilot program at outdoor gear and clothing retailer REI's corporate offices. The goal: develop a presentation for senior REI executives detailing how the company could appeal to young consumers.

The week was a success. Besides nailing the presentation, the budding professionals gained tangible workplace experience and newfound confidence.

"The intention is to obliterate the statistic that 53 percent of college grads are underemployed or unemployed," says Hamilton, Koru's CEO. "We're fixing a problem for employers, too, because it turns out that employers struggle to figure out who the right hires are when people don't have a lot of experience."

To develop Koru's employer-embedded training programs, Hamilton and Jarrett closed $4.5 million in seed financing at the end of 2013, followed by an $8 million Series A round early this year. Hamilton was no stranger to fundraising, having cofounded online small business retailer Onvia in 1997, when she raised more than $200 million in investment capital. Koru's fundraising efforts were highly calculated, from timing and pitch strategy to investors courted and sums sought.

"Fundraising is really an art and a science," Hamilton says. "You have to be thinking, 'How many rounds? How much runway do I want? What do I need to do to be able to prove the next milestone?'"

The next section talks about how she and Jarrett secured $12.5 million for Koru in 18 months.

The Hunt for Seed Funding

The founders approached a small set of prospective seed investors in September 2013, certain they had a winning idea in a multibillion-dollar market. But conviction gets you only so far. Without any business metrics or revenue under their belt, the pair had to make a convincing case.

To do so, their pitch deck leaned heavily on stats. They cited research showing that $150 billion is spent in the U.S. each year on college tuition, yet 70 percent of college grads have degrees they can't apply in the workforce. Employers spend $60 billion annually to hire entry-level talent but complain that 20 to 30 percent of their hires are bad ones, with 53 percent of employers saying they can't find qualified candidates at all. Enter Koru, which strives to bridge this gap by creating hirable young professionals with proven experience.

Hamilton and Jarrett emphasized the partnerships they'd begun building with employers such as REI, Zulily, and Trupanion, as well as top liberal arts colleges and public and private universities. The founders also touted their own resumes: Hamilton, who saw Onvia through its IPO in 2000, later served as COO of global education nonprofit World Learning and global director of educator strategy and marketing at Microsoft. Jarrett, a Harvard MBA and Koru's chief learning officer, spent seven years heading higher-education initiatives at the Bill & Melinda Gates Foundation.

The Deal

The pair's goal was to raise at least $1 million to prove their concept, which they predicted would take 18 months. But investor interest was so great that Koru raised $4.5 million in roughly two months "at a very good valuation," Hamilton says, pointing out that this was a priced round rather than a convertible-note or debt-based round. Venture capital firms Battery Ventures, based in Waltham, Massachusetts, and Maveron in Seattle led the round.

Maveron invests only in consumer startups. "If a company does not have an opportunity to build an iconic consumer brand and become a household name, we're not interested," says Maveron general partner Clayton Lewis, who serves as a Koru board member.

Funding participants also included First Round Capital, Andreessen Horowitz, QueensBridge Venture Partners (founded by rapper Nas, who reached out to Koru unsolicited), and 10 angel investors. Most were people the founders already knew or with whom they secured introductions through their network. "We were really helped by the fact that we weren't wandering in off the street asking for funding," Jarrett recalls.

Once funded, the duo was faced with hitting the milestones they had outlined in their seed-round pitch. That meant expanding their hands-on training programs to three weeks, hiring instructors, and launching programs in Seattle, Boston, and San Francisco by early 2015. It also meant attracting college grads willing to pay the program's fee, which starts at $2,749. And it meant securing enough employer and higher-education partners to make the program a success. (Partner employers pay an undisclosed placement fee upon hiring Koru graduates.)

They succeeded on all counts. Demand for Koru's experiential training programs was high. Partnerships were flourishing, too, with 20 schools and more than 40 employers onboard.

The phase was completed months earlier than Hamilton and Jarrett had predicted. Rather than risk running out of operating capital, the founders rolled up their sleeves and embarked on another round of fundraising.

Landing the Series A

Here's where the heavy lifting began. Raising Series A funds, Hamilton says, "is a much higher bar, and you have to show results."

A pitch demonstrating Koru's short track record required hard numbers and testimonials from satisfied graduates and partner companies. The concise, 12-slide deck also required a bit more polish. "It's important to pay a designer," Hamilton notes.

Among Koru's selling points: The startup had successfully trained hundreds of handpicked college graduates, with 85 percent of them landing "meaningful" jobs with Koru's partner companies afterward. The company also boasted a 70 to 90 percent net promoter score, with an overwhelming majority of grads recommending the program to friends, helping keep customer acquisition costs down. Revenue was strong and growing exponentially. (Hamilton declined to share specific numbers.)

Other highlights included Koru's contractual agreements with high-growth employers such as LinkedIn, Yelp, and Zillow and premier colleges such as Georgetown, Brown, and Vassar. New executives hailing from the highest ranks of Amazon and Yahoo! had joined the Koru team, as had an impressive list of advisors, including a vice president of recruiting from LinkedIn, as well as a bestselling author / expert-in-residence at Harvard.

The Deal

Koru sought meetings with a dozen top VC firms focused on technology and education. Hamilton and Jarrett worked with their seed investors to target the right contacts at each firm and obtain introductions as needed. "You don't want to shop your deal too much," Hamilton says. "You want to be really targeted."

Maveron, which led the round with an investment of more than $3 million, had already funded two edutech startups, Capella Education and Course Hero. City Light Capital in New York, the round's second-biggest investor at $2 million, had been involved with 2U, an edutech startup with a successful 2014 IPO. Battery Ventures, First Round Capital, and Trilogy Equity Partners also participated in the $8 million round.

Most of the investors were contacts the founders had known for five to ten years. That's the way to go, says Maveron's Lewis, who initially met Hamilton when she hired him to join Onvia's executive team in 1999.

"We're really laser-focused on backing individuals," Lewis says. "On average, we know the entrepreneurs we back in our core investments for a year and a half. For us, it's about the relationships."

Next Steps

Hamilton expects Koru's earnings and customer base to increase every year. Now, she says, the test is to keep scaling; she wants to see how Koru's first three geographic markets do before speculating on when the company will expand into other cities.

In the meantime, the company is using the capital raised to expand market reach and develop technology. To that end, Koru has beefed up its engineering and product development staff, bringing the company to more than 20 full-time employees.

Hamilton anticipates a Series B round at some point. The idea, she explains, is to ensure that the company always has a year or two of capital on hand. "You're always fundraising. It's a never-ending process in many ways. That's why one of the most important skills of an entrepreneur is being able to raise money."

Countdown to VC

Every deal is different. But in general, the funding timeline can be distilled to 10 milestones that happen in two rounds of funding, known as the seed round and the Series A round.

Seed Round

Typically $500,000 to $1.5 million to sustain the business for 6 to 18 months.

1. Develop your business plan and pitch deck. (Time to complete: two to four months)
2. Develop a target list of angels and early-stage VCs to pitch. (Two weeks)

3.   Shop your idea around. (Six to eight weeks)
4.   Interested angels and VCs conduct due diligence on the founders and the idea's potential to disrupt. (Six to eight weeks)
5.   Interested investors will offer a term sheet and give you time to sign. (15 to 30 days)

Series A Round

Typically up to $20 million to sustain the business for 12 to 18 months.

1.   Once you've been operational for two to three quarters and have gained traction with customers, update your business plan and pitch deck. (Two to four weeks)
2.   Update your list of potential investors to include later-stage VCs. (Two weeks)
3.   Preview your Series A pitch deck with your seed-round investors to get their feedback before you pitch later-stage VCs. (Six to eight weeks)
4.   Secure Series A funds from your seed investors and then target, pitch, and secure additional later-stage investors, ideally at a higher valuation than your seed round. (Six to eight weeks)
5.   Twelve to 18 months later, the goal is that you'll have broken even or be in shape to raise a Series B financing round.

Finding Investors through LinkedIn

Dave Gowel raised $3 million in the first three years of RockTech, a Cambridge, Massachusetts–based enterprise training platform for cloud technologies that he helmed from 2010 to 2016. Of the 29 angel investors he brought onboard during that time, all had one thing in common: "Every investor relationship I have was influenced by LinkedIn," says Gowel.

"A compelling example of this came when one of my investors listed his affiliation with RockTech on LinkedIn, and then another angel who saw that update contacted me," Gowel continues. "The latter angel had a very strong respect for my investor who had updated his profile, and [he] became an investor within six months—he even brought in another angel to invest with him."

Thanks to the U.S. Securities and Exchange Commission lifting the ban on general solicitation for investors, LinkedIn has become a potential mother lode for identifying and pitching investors. But it's a nuanced and regulated game.

"I don't think a general solicitation as a first contact is the way to go," Gowel says. Instead, he and others recommend using LinkedIn as a recon tool to improve real-world interactions with potential investors. The following sections discuss how.

Embrace the Advanced Search

If you're not clicking the "Advanced" link next to the site's search bar and hunting by industry, company, location, alma mater, groups you belong to, or specific keywords of your choosing, you're wasting your time, says Gowel, who is also the author of *The Power in a Link: Open Doors, Close Deals, and Change the Way You Do Business Using LinkedIn.*

"There are 300-million-plus people on LinkedIn," he says. "Advanced searches help you cut through the clutter and zero in on the right people to meet."

Next, follow a potential investor's company page. Join any relevant LinkedIn groups to which your target belongs. Scour his or her profile and posts to familiarize yourself with the person's portfolio, investment approach, likes, and dislikes, says Milwaukee entrepreneur Seth Knapp, who's sussing out investors for his social marketing app, Chitter. "Reaching out to an investor without doing any homework tells him everything he needs to know about you—none of it good," he explains.

Vet and Be Vetted

Resist the urge to ping investors who sound like a good fit right away. Instead, ask mutual contacts for insights about them, Gowel advises. You don't want to partner with an investor who's known for being difficult or one who doesn't meet the SEC's definition of an accredited investor.

If you do decide to move forward, don't contact an investor cold; an introduction through a mutual contact can catapult you to the top of the correspondence slush pile.

"The one thing you can't fabricate is a strong relationship," Gowel says. Plus, he adds, a mutual acquaintance may know how and when that investor prefers to be contacted.

Be Patient

Partnerships aren't built overnight. "Your deck and any other information you send over will fall on far less deaf ears if you patiently develop a relationship with the investor," Knapp says.

Of course, most angels won't end up investing, no matter how much they love your pitch, warns Brandon Bruce, COO and cofounder of Cirrus Insight, which sells a software add-on to Salesforce. But a carefully cultivated relationship can lead to market intel, strategic advice, and, most importantly, referrals to other potential investors.

The Fine Print

Despite the SEC's loosened regulations, there are still rules for soliciting investors. Before you start hitting up your LinkedIn network to publicize your capital raise, consult an attorney to make sure your pitch is legal and your paperwork has been filed with the SEC.

You'll also need to familiarize yourself with the SEC definition of "accredited investor"—someone who has $200,000 or more in annual income or $300,000 in annual household income or who exceeds $1 million in net worth, excluding primary residence. Keep in mind it is your responsibility to make sure the investors are accredited. If they're not associated with an angel funding group or known to be accredited, you may have to ask them to provide copies of their tax returns to prove it.

Look at Your LinkedIn Profile First

Louis Beryl remembers how tough it was to get credit when he was in his 20s, even with a solid resume and a spotless financial history. "If you're low risk, you deserve a low interest rate," insists the Harvard MBA and former Wall Streeter.

When he became a partner at venture capital firm Andreessen Horowitz in 2012, he hoped to find a financial technology startup involved in building what he calls "the modern bank for the next generation of consumers." He didn't. So, in 2013, he founded Earnest, an online lender of low-cost personal loans to financially sound applicants. His cofounder was Benjamin Hutchinson, a finance exec who had worked at the U.K.'s HM Treasury during the banking meltdown.

San Francisco–based Earnest has launched in 19 states and closed $15 million in financing from Andreessen Horowitz, Atlas Venture, Collaborative Fund, First Round Capital, and Maveron, as well as more than 15 angel investors. Earnest has loaned approximately $2 million to young people who need cash for moving costs, weddings, home repairs, vacations, furniture, and the like.

The lender assesses each applicant as an individual, not a number, he explains. "It's not just, 'Do you have this credit score?' Or, 'Do you make this amount of money?' For us, it's really about, 'Are you financially responsible?'"

The company's underwriting software pulls data from the applicants' LinkedIn profile and financial accounts, evaluating education, work history, salary, savings, cash flow, and earning potential, and Earnest staffers review each prospective client by phone. Loans are typically fulfilled within 48 hours of application.

Earnest recently began offering larger loans, longer repayment periods, and both lower and higher interest-rate loans "in order to serve more people," according to Beryl. One-, two- and three-year loans are available, ranging from $2,000 to $30,000 and from 4.25 percent to 9.25 percent APR. The company charges no origination, prepayment, or other fees. "These aren't teaser rates," Beryl stresses.

The Earnest founders felt it was essential to partner with VCs that supported their commitment to customer value and weren't just looking for a quick exit. Like all the company's investors and advisors, Bill Trenchard, partner at First Round Capital, which contributed an undisclosed amount, was onboard with Earnest's mission.

"It was a gap in the marketplace that seemed wide open," Trenchard says, citing the availability of customer data and pointing out that traditional banks are too mired in regulation to take risks. San Francisco–

based Trenchard has also invested in online lending platforms OnDeck and Lending Club.

Since raising the $15 million, Earnest has grown from a team of five to more than 125. Most of the staff is made up of software engineers, designers, and data scientists. In addition, a "client happiness" team works the phones, answering questions about the application process and helping existing customers. "That's the team that's most likely to grow the fastest as we expand," Beryl says.

Earnest offers loans in 39 states plus D.C. and is shooting for all 50 in the coming years. Keeping customer costs affordable throughout will remain a priority. "We're building a 100-year company," Beryl says. "We want our clients' happiness to be so good that their grandkids will be our customers."

Five Essentials for Raising Your Growth Round of Funding by Matt Straz

Matt Straz is the founder and CEO of the HR platform Namely (www.namely.com). This section, written by him from his point of view, gives his advice on raising a growth round of funding:

While there are many thousands of people and firms that can provide money to get a startup going, far fewer entities, perhaps just a couple dozen depending on the business, can fund a Series B or C. I raised my Series B round in 2014, and here is what I learned.

Kiss a Lot of Frogs

Finding the right venture firm requires meeting many of them, since most will pass on the investment no matter how well the company is doing. When I realize there isn't a fit, I often break up with the firm quickly, sometimes emailing a nice "no thanks" note as I leave their office. This makes founders feel more in control of a process that is riddled with rejection.

Define Growth

Many venture firms claim to be "growth"-stage investors, but that term can mean a lot of things to different people. When receiving a call from a VC firm, establish up front if they have an established minimum revenue or annual "run rate" in order to make an investment. Some investors will want to see a $5 million to $10 million run rate before they invest. Others won't care and will base their decision on how fast the company is growing and if they like the market.

Be Quantitative

Once a B round is received, things become less about the founder and more about the business and its metrics.

For example, if the company is a SaaS (Software as a Service), deliver highly detailed reports on things like monthly recurring revenue (MRR), annual contract value (ACV), and customer churn. If the company is a B2C, show high levels of user growth and engagement.

Whatever the metrics for the company's particular industry, have them at the ready when the fundraising process begins.

Show It

At this stage, investors expect significant growth in the months and years following their investment. For example, if the company is a SaaS company, show how it will grow at least three times annually in the years following the investment.

Ultimately, investors want to know how fast the company can get to $100 million in revenue so it can IPO or be acquired. If this is not achievable, then think twice about raising a Series B.

It Ain't Over Until It's Over

Even if a VC firm is interested in funding the company next round, there are things to tend to once a term sheet is received.

Due diligence is typically a formality involving a lot of paperwork being sent back and forth, so have good financial records in place. Also, the public announcement of a U.S. fundraising must happen within 30 days of the closing, as it needs to be filed with the federal government.

Be sure to work with a good PR firm or have a solid relationship with a tech writer to tell the company's story. Don't let hard work be ruined by a poor or muddled fundraising story.

Securing a growth-stage investment is rare. Most startups never get to this point. But with the right metrics and approach, it can absolutely happen!

Acing Your Pitch to Investors

Your pitch is the single thing that could either get your business off the ground or plunge your idea into eternal oblivion. It matters.

The rule of thumb for investors is that for every 100 investments they make, only 10 will go big.

Let's take that rule a step further. For every 1,000 pitches an investor hears, he or she will fund only 100 of them. Statistically, the odds for success are not great. You can beat the statistics, however, by crafting a pitch that turns heads and gets funded.

What are the ingredients of an ultra-compelling, irresistible, outstanding, and unforgettable pitch?

Take Only 10 Minutes

Timing is critical. The less time your pitch takes, the better. A brilliant idea means nothing unless you can distill it to a few moments of sheer power. The more concise you can be, the more effective you will be. Here are a few timing pointers:

- If you say you'll take "only X minutes," take at least one minute less.
- If you are told, "You only have X minutes to pitch," take at least five minutes less.
- If you say, "One last thing," make sure it's truly the last thing.
- Move at a good pace. Don't rush at the end.
- If you're using slides, don't stay on one slide for more than three minutes.

Here's the great thing about taking 10 minutes. If the investors are really interested, they'll ask questions. If they're not, you will have saved them (and yourself) some time.

Turn Your Pitch into a Story

Storytelling is a scientifically proven way to capture a listener's attention and hold it. Besides, it makes your pitch unforgettable. Investors are bored with spreadsheets, valuations, and numbers. If they want that information, they can get it. What you can offer that no term sheet can convey is the story and pathos behind your startup. Everyone loves a good story, even the most data-driven investor.

So tell your story and tell it right. You're bound to gain attention, and the funding will follow.

Be Laser-Focused

Investors' time is their most valuable asset. If you convey respect for their time, they will interpret that as your willingness to treat their funding with respect.

Because time is important, you need to develop an absolute focus on the core components of your pitch, detailed in the following tips.

Explain Exactly What Your Product or Service Is

Show your potential investors a picture of or give them the actual product to handle. Be careful not to drone endlessly on about your product. Honestly, investors don't care about your product as much as they care about the money your product will make. The sooner you get to the money, the better.

Explain Exactly What Is Unique about Your Product or Service

If you are not producing or providing anything different from the run-of-the-mill widget, don't even go to the meeting. Go back to your drawing board, and design something better.

Explain Exactly Who Your Target Audience Is

Use demographic and psychographic features to pinpoint your customers. Show investors a picture of a customer along with relevant data points.

Explain Exactly How You Intend to Acquire These Customers

Business success comes down to marketing. If you have a marketing idea, method, technique, or process, this is your chance to showcase it. Contrary to pithy maxims, great products don't sell themselves. You sell the product. To be persuaded, investors have to see an airtight strategy for getting the product to market.

Most VCs are well aware of the advantages of digital marketing and won't take a second glance at a product that isn't backed by a tactical plan for online marketing.

Explain Your Revenue Model

Investors invest because they want to make a return on that investment. An investor will care about your pitch if you can answer this question: How will my company make you rich?

The answer, in investor-speak, is your revenue model. Specifically identify which type of revenue model you are embracing, and how you intend to apply it.

Be Wildly Enthusiastic

Whatever you think of *Shark Tank* or investor Barbara Corcoran, you can't argue with her insight into pitching a business idea: "My whole focus is on trying to size up the entrepreneur. I am looking at how much wild enthusiasm they genuinely have for their product. You can't fake passion."

A good technique for increasing your energy level is to add about 50 percent more energy than you feel comfortable with. Entrepreneurs must crawl out of their comfort zone.

Wild enthusiasm will not obscure your sophistication, insight, integrity, and realism. It will only enhance it.

Dress to Kill

People judge a person by the way he or she looks. That may be unfair, and you may resent it, but you're not going to overcome this natural human tendency. The thousand bucks you spend on a new suit will pay for itself a thousand times over when you secure the funding you need. So don't skimp.

Practice Your Pitch

And then practice it again. And again.

Anticipate Questions and Answer Them Ahead of Time

If an investor is interested, he or she will ask more questions. Be ready for them. By formulating skillful and persuasive answers to the tough questions, you will demonstrate the panoply of abilities and traits that investors love to see.

Show Them the Exit

Here's the clincher on a killer pitch: an exit strategy. Starstruck entrepreneurs usually overlook this critical component when they're pitching. They're so sold on their sexy product that they cannot conceive there will ever be a need for an exit.

Every investor wants to make a lot of money in a short amount of time. What is a "short amount of time"? A five-year benchmark is a safe time frame. Your plan and pitch, then, should explicitly answer the investor's unstated question: How will this make me a lot of money in five years?

The answer is your exit strategy. Is it an IPO? An acquisition? Licensing? To answer "sales revenue or valuation" is to shipwreck your plan from the start. Investors want big payoffs, not marginal returns. They want to retire comfortably on a big yacht, not get their money back in a little equity package.

Bottom line: The goal of a successful pitch is to have investors begging to invest in your company. Sure, that sounds too good to be true, but it is possible. When you successfully deliver on what an investor wants, you will have a truly irresistible pitch.

Challenges Women Face When Raising Venture Capital

Women start more than 50 percent of the businesses in the U.S., but account for just a small fraction of the companies that receive venture capital funding. There are a few issues that hold women back from major sources of funding.

Venture capital funding, particularly at the early stages, is the most robust in industries like technology and biotechnology. These industries generally attract more men than women. A tech startup might be able to raise substantial venture capital on merely an idea or at least an early-stage prototype. However, a consumer products venture—an industry where many women entrepreneurs tend to start—needs to have substantial revenue and financial metrics to attract venture capitalists focused on those industries. Nontech service businesses—another arena that attracts a lot of women—have very few early-stage investors.

If you are a woman thinking about starting a business, consider what type of business you are starting to give yourself an edge in raising capital. Also think about how you can transform your idea into a tech play. You could argue that Grubhub, the online restaurant delivery company, is really a service business, but they have firmly positioned themselves as a technology company. Do the same to attract early-stage investment.

Thinking Bigger

Women tend to be more conservative and more risk averse when it comes to making business projections. While this creates a better risk-adjusted return for women CEOs, according to *Shark Tank*'s Kevin O'Leary, it can also hurt you in the capital-raising process.

Angel and venture capital investors want to invest in opportunities with huge potential and a management team with a big vision. So being conservative, while theoretically prudent, doesn't play well in the early-stage capital game. It makes the opportunity look too small or the management team seem as if they don't have the gravitas to pull off something extraordinary. With investors always discounting your projections anyway, you need to be able to authentically and realistically defend how you can make your company grow by leaps and bounds.

Don't Play it Too Safe

One of the best ways to get a leg up on funding is by having someone in your network make a direct introduction to funding sources. This helps get investors more focused on you, as you have had some level of verification from a connection, plus the obligation that comes from following through on an introduction from a contact.

Women too often focus their networking on women's-only groups. While there are a number of great angel and venture capital funds spearheaded by women or that focus on women, women make up only 4 percent of the decision-makers in venture capital.

Cindy Bates, vice president of U.S. Small-to-Midsize Business at Microsoft, said "While many women have faced an uphill battle in their entrepreneurial endeavors, the challenges often have fostered new strengths and determination that are integral to ferreting out financial support from potential investors. Not broadening your network as a woman when seeking funding means that you may miss out on the lion's share of funding sources."

Fundraising is a numbers game, meaning that you want to get in front of as many sources of funding as practicable. Don't do yourself a disservice by focusing too narrowly.

What VCs Want and Look For

What do venture capitalists want? For entrepreneurs in search of funding, this is the perennial question.

Dominating the investment marketplace over the past decade have been tech companies, including internet, social media, and artificial intelligence. Also hot are mobile, telecom, health care, financial, education, and consumer startups.

So, what will be hot next? We asked some leading VCs to put their money where their mouths were, filling us in on the sectors that excite them most—and those likely to score major financing in the months and years ahead.

Cybersecurity

Take corporate and consumer concerns about data integrity, add ongoing developments in mobile and cloud technology, and you get a scorching market.

"The sophistication of the bad guys has increased," says Theresia Gouw, cofounder and managing partner of Aspect Ventures, a San Francisco firm that invests in digital marketplaces, security, health IT, and analytics. "That, coupled with massive change in technology infrastructure, is creating huge opportunity. It's like a perfect storm."

Consider Exabeam, a big-data security company that has raised $35 million in financing, including contributions from Aspect Ventures. The company employs user-behavior analytics to detect cyberattacks that rely on stolen credentials. "You've got to think about users," says Gouw, who has been investing in security companies for 15 years. "Most of the big hacks that you've read about, everything from the Sony hack to the Target hack, are bad guys getting users' credentials."

Sean Flynn, managing director of Shasta Ventures—a Silicon Valley firm that makes Series A investments in enterprise software, consumer internet companies, and connected hardware devices—gets excited about mobile security, especially with so many employees using their own devices at work. In early 2015, Shasta contributed to an $8 million investment round in Skycure, a solution that protects bring-your-own and employer-issued mobile devices in the workplace from internal and external security threats. "We think that most enterprises are quite exposed," Flynn says. "And we feel like that's a really big opportunity."

On-Demand Platforms

Startups that focus on quality assurance and smooth transactions are the name of the game, says Flynn, whose Shasta Ventures invested in Turo, a national peer-to-peer car-rental platform. Turo screens renters, provides various levels of insurance, and offers 24/7 roadside assistance.

"It's tapping into underutilized assets and building a product around that marketplace so it's not just a free-for-all," Flynn says.

Maha Ibrahim, general partner at global VC firm Canaan Partners, which focuses on technology and health care, expects on-demand startups to add more premium, white-glove services in the near future. As an example, she points to onefinestay, an Airbnb for upscale homes that vets listings and offers concierge services. Another example from Canaan's portfolio: the RealReal, a luxury-brand consignment platform that vets all goods listed on the site, provides high-end photos of them, and ships them to buyers.

"It's a way of capturing more money from that premium user," says Ibrahim, who expects the trend to proliferate throughout the travel, fashion, and food-delivery sectors.

Consumer Health Care

Technology companies that make medical treatment more efficient for patients are another good bet. Shasta Ventures has invested in Doctor On Demand, which lets users consult board-certified physicians, psychologists, and lactation consultants over video call.

Also hot right now: wellness platforms that doctors, insurers, and employers can offer their patients and employees to help them stay healthy or recover from a medical setback.

Aspect Ventures' Gouw credits mobility, the consumerization of health care, and the Affordable Care Act with the growth of the sector. Case in point: Vida, a platform her firm invested in that pairs individuals with a coach who counsels them on fitness, nutrition, and general well-being while monitoring their vital signs.

Sharon Vosmek, CEO of Astia, a San Francisco–based nonprofit dedicated to identifying and promoting women as high-growth entrepreneurs, sees innovations in traditionally underfunded areas, like women's health and reproductive health, as a growing market. Astia Angels, a global network of angel investors, backs select Astia companies across the sectors of tech, life science, medical device, consumer products, and health and wellness.

"We plan to double down on those companies that actually understand that the female health-care market is a large and expanding market," Vosmek says. A few examples from the Astia Angels portfolio: nVision Medical, a medical-device startup tackling female infertility; Sandstone Diagnostics, which has developed a male fertility tracker; and Naya Health, which makes a smart breast pump for nursing mothers.

Services for the Underserved

It has become smart business to develop education, employment, and lending work-arounds. "People are looking to alternative pathways to get to school and to get that four-year degree, but they're also looking for alternative ways to get the type of education they need in order to get the kind of jobs they want," says William Crowder of the Comcast Ventures Catalyst Fund, the telecom giant's $20 million New York–based venture fund for early-stage tech startups led by minority entrepreneurs. As an example, Crowder points to Catalyst Fund portfolio company Quad Learning, which works with community colleges to offer affordable education for students earning a bachelor's degree.

Dan Levitan, cofounder and general partner of Maveron, a consumer-only VC firm based in Seattle and San Francisco, shares these sentiments. "We think that the whole jobs market and 'How do you get liberal arts people jobs?' is a very big idea," he says.

Besides investing in educational startups Koru and General Assembly, Maveron has championed Earnest, an online lender that offers low-interest personal loans and student loan refinancing to fiscally responsible borrowers. "The lowest rate that Earnest has on a student loan is like 2 percent for highly qualified buyers," Levitan says.

Robotics and Drones

Robotic toys and vacuum cleaners may be all the rage, but Shasta Ventures is more enthused about robots for enterprise. "You can build really functional products that make companies much more efficient," Flynn says. Fetch Robotics, one of Shasta's portfolio companies, has a suite of robots for warehouses that enables businesses to pack and ship products in a more streamlined way.

Then there are drones. Although they've been touted as a solution for delivering items from ecommerce companies, regulatory concerns persist. Other applications are likely to gain ground first. "I think we'll see a first wave of drone companies targeting image applications, whether that's taking pictures of houses or surveying land," says Brian Wilcove, a partner at Artiman Ventures. His fund has looked at a couple dozen drone startup deals in the past year. Other possible uses: monitoring bridges, cell towers, and dangerous locations.

CHAPTER 10

Considering VC Alternatives and Other Investors

Traditional angels and VCs aren't the only games in town. This chapter talks about some other viable investors you may want to consider.

If a company is more established and ready to exchange equity for capital, there are additional funding avenues beyond venture capital firms. Before spending months and months chasing venture capitalists (who only fund less than 1 percent of U.S. companies), it's a good idea to find out if the company's state of residence is one of the growing number that have approved intrastate crowdfunding. Or consider a Rule 506 of Regulation D private offering, a direct public offering, or even a Regulation A funding path, depending on the company's stage of growth.

When to Say No to Venture Capital: Q&A with Qualtrics' Ryan Smith

Ryan Smith knew he wanted to build a company he could grow over the long haul. So, rather than race to find financiers in 2002, the cofounder and CEO of Qualtrics spent four years bootstrapping his enterprise survey provider from his dad's basement.

That low overhead helped the Provo, Utah, startup reach profitability almost immediately. As the company grew year by year, venture capitalists started circling, reaching critical mass during year five. Smith says he fielded roughly 100 calls from venture capitalists and investment groups before he finally agreed to a deal in 2012.

What drew them to Qualtrics? A sound and profitable business model, according to Bryan Schreier, a partner at Sequoia Capital, who eventually succeeded, along with Accel, in funding Smith to the tune of $70 million. "[Bootstrapping longer] focuses the company on creating a healthy business model at a very early stage," Schreier says. "It's hard to create a viable business model five years down the road. It's much easier if you're focused on making money from the start."

Qualtrics has enjoyed triple-digit growth. A leader in experience management (XM), the company's worldwide customers include 85 percent of the Fortune 100. It boasts 3 million users.

Entrepreneur spoke with Smith about the many ways Qualtrics benefited from waiting to raise VC and what other startups can learn from his experience:

Entrepreneur: *How did waiting help?*

Smith: We really wanted to nail it before we scaled it, which we did. There are some companies, like an app, where they need to go full speed on the scaling up as fast as possible. But for most companies that have a pretty big opportunity like us, I think nailing the product and business model is critical. I think if a company doesn't have its core figured out, it could be really difficult to find it when there's $20 million sitting in the bank that has to be spent now.

Entrepreneur: *How did you decide which VCs to partner with?*

Smith: Our philosophy has been that one and one needs to equal five. Just because someone called us and said that they wanted to invest in us didn't mean we had to stop everything and say yes. We wanted partners who were as excited about the opportunity as we were, who were excited about us, who were even excited about Utah.

We were in a position to pick the firm, and we had time to build the relationship before signing an agreement. I think that many early funding scenarios are akin to getting married after a first date. Not knowing what they're getting into is where people struggle.

Entrepreneur: *What advice can you offer startups thinking about VC?*

Smith: Ask yourself why. If you're in a "scale it" phase, I think funding can do a ton of good. If you're in a "nail it" phase, I think that's where you see companies thrash around and a lot of them fail. If you're thinking about taking money, talk to portfolio companies. Talk to companies who have taken funding from [VCs].

I believe that people need to bet on themselves more. What I've seen is that if you're a great company, and you've got what it takes to take it the distance, then you're going to have more and more opportunities the farther you go along. Trust me, they aren't going to go away.

Why the VC Game Is Attracting a Whole New Set of Players

In 2015, Boston-based 3-D printing company Voxel8 raised $12 million in Series A funding. Included in the windfall were contributions from Autodesk's Spark Investment Fund—the software company's $100 million 3-D printing investment initiative—and In-Q-Tel, the CIA's venture fund for intelligence-related innovations.

Wireless intercom company Nucleus scored more than $1.6 million in seed investments in 2015, $100,000 of which came from Philadelphia's

$6 million StartUp PHL fund, which makes equity investments in local entrepreneurs. And Back to the Roots, a San Francisco–area sustainable food company, raised $650,000 from ICA Fund Good Jobs, a $2.53 million philanthropic venture fund focused on job creation.

These unconventional VC groups aren't anomalies. In recent years, corporations, municipalities, university alumni groups, and philanthropic groups with agendas beyond reaping financial rewards have jumped into the equity financing game.

Michael Collins, cofounder and lead manager of Launch Angels, a VC firm that creates and manages university alumni investment funds, credits technological innovations with the rise in nontraditional VC groups. With geographically diverse investment committees easily able to meet by Skype or Google Hangouts, managing alumni investment teams is a cinch, Collins explains.

What's more, the ubiquity of tech startups—and the decreased financial barrier to entry—has prompted Philadelphia and Detroit, among other cities, to begin offering venture capital in an effort to boost economic development, create jobs, and attract young people, says Archna Sahay, Philadelphia's director of entrepreneurial investment.

"The existence of early-stage capital is missing in the ecosystem," Sahay says. And with traditional venture funding not always available to young companies, it makes sense for entrepreneurs to consider the alternatives.

Of course, most hybrid venture funds come with their own set of caveats. The trick to accepting alternative VC is ensuring that your goals mesh with those of your investors. When Nucleus founder Jonathan Frankel accepted six figures from StartUp PHL, he agreed his company would remain in Philadelphia for 18 months. Likewise, Back to the Roots had to upgrade its employee benefits package before ICA Fund Good Jobs would consider leading a $2 million funding round. "They wouldn't invest until we provided health care for the whole team," says Back to the Roots cofounder Alejandro Velez, noting that his company had eight employees at the time.

Some alternative VCs have a more sophisticated understanding of the startup world than others and, as a result, can offer more useful advice and introductions. Consider StartUp PHL. By teaming up with traditional VC firm First Round Capital, the city of Philadelphia has substantially upped the mentorship ante for the entrepreneurs it funds.

For Frankel, the willingness of First Round Capital's Josh Kopelman to weigh in with the occasional suggestion has been a bonus for Nucleus. "There are very few people who write you a check and then just disappear," he says. "Either they're checking in too frequently and offering bad advice or, like StartUp PHL, they're available when necessary to lend an ear and a hand. People should just be careful to determine which type of investor they're taking money from."

The Rise of Corporate Venture Capital

All venture capital is aimed at funding promising young companies, but whereas a traditional venture capital firm raises money primarily from institutional investors and high-net-worth individuals, corporate venture capital uses cash reserves from a parent company to fund new endeavors. This difference is significant, because it means more external pressure is typically put on independent venture capital firms to generate above-average returns. Since corporate ventures are typically considered R&D alternatives, expenses are already built into the business structure, and separate revenue-generating businesses help offset any corporate venture capital losses. That's a safety net traditional venture capital firms don't have.

Corporate venture capital efforts also have the advantage of involvement with startups at the early stages, when they can most benefit from access to a large, established customer base; credibility through brand association; and a larger network of partner companies and advisors.

Corporate venture capital efforts can make good co-investment partners with traditional venture capital firms because each brings different expertise to the table. Venture capital firms have the drive and know-how to realize financial results, while corporate venture capital groups provide industry knowledge and a talent pool.

Corporations have been actively investing in venture capital since the mid-1960s, when the venture capital industry itself was just emerging. But as more corporations become involved, the emphasis on how to build the next generation of businesses could shift away from high valuations and quick exits to creating a nurturing environment for bigger and better ideas.

Corporate venture capital is picking up speed in the investment industry, as large companies start setting aside funds for external investment in fledgling companies or startups. Tech giants like Intel, Dell, and AMD all have strong track records with their proprietary funds, and more companies like Microsoft and Salesforce are entering the venture fund game. Hundreds of corporate venture funds have started, bringing the investment of corporate venture capital to $7.5 billion in 2015, according to Global Corporate Venturing.

Corporate venture capital also lets large companies operate on a smaller scale, which lets them innovate faster, conduct research on disruptive technologies, and preempt competitors. And it's an efficient way for companies to explore potential acquisition targets. Data from CrunchBase shows that about one-third of corporate venture–backed startups have been acquired versus one-tenth of startups with funding only from private venture capital. Corporations can use their venture arms to influence their industry's ecosystem by identifying new markets and building up their existing businesses.

The Deal with Revenue Sharing Deals: Royalty Loans

John Stewart knew his company needed a hefty cash infusion to transition from a cloud services provider to a software provider. Without physical assets to borrow against, a bank loan was out of the question; venture capital wasn't an option, either. "We were too late for angel funding and too early for growth funding," says Stewart, CEO of Charlotte, North Carolina–based MapAnything.

His solution: borrow $1 million from Lighter Capital, a Seattle financing firm that specializes in revenue-based deals—which focus on sharing a percentage of the company's future revenues with the investor, instead of an ownership stake, until a predefined financial target is reached—with small businesses poised for big growth. Rather than forfeit equity or repay a fixed monthly amount, MapAnything pays Lighter Capital 7 percent of its monthly revenue. The more the company makes in a given month, the faster it repays the debt.

Thanks to the money borrowed, which MapAnything sank into sales and marketing, the company turned its business model on its head. In

2012, MapAnything had revenue of $1.9 million, $600,000 of which was in software sales, Stewart says. In 2013, the company made $4 million, with $3.6 million of that in software deals.

Lighter Capital is among a handful of U.S. firms offering five-, six-, and seven-figure revenue or royalty financing to young companies with high gross margins. "There are lots of great companies out there that could easily be $10 million to $30 million businesses, but not $1 billion businesses," says BJ Lackland, CEO of Lighter Capital. "Thus, they have a hard time attracting venture capital. We fill that gap."

If you want to pursue this type of financing, here's what you need to do:

Demonstrate Growth Potential

Financiers want to see proof of your profit margins and growth potential; the same goes for healthy cash flow. Lighter Capital, for example, wants at least 12 to 24 months of solid financial documentation, with minimum revenue of $15,000 a month. "We don't require a company to be profitable," Lackland says, "but we want to see where they have a path to profitability."

Show How You'll Use the Money

If you can't specify how you'll use the funds, you're not ready for a revenue or royalty loan. These lenders want assurance that you'll use their money for growth-oriented activities. "Marketing and sales are a good use of the funds," Stewart says. The typical Lighter Capital customer uses funds to hire a vice president of sales, launch a marketing initiative, or finish and launch a product, according to Lackland.

Make Sure the Numbers Work

A revenue or royalty loan is worthless if repaying it completely hobbles your cash flow. For Tracey Noonan, co-owner of Wicked Good Cupcakes, a $75,000 royalty deal with a private investor in 2013 made sense: Sales were exponential, and she needed money to move to a bigger facility and buy packaging in bulk. The Boston-area entrepreneur paid off the loan in 72 days and reduced the royalties paid on her signature $6.95 cupcake in a jar from $1 per unit to 45 cents, in perpetuity.

Although the permanence of such an arrangement may sound onerous, Noonan is thrilled: "What we pay back now is the equivalent of a 12 percent equity stake, a small cut that we never would have gotten from an investor as a new company."

Think about Mentorship

It's not just about who can cut you the best deal. "You're going to want an investor that can help you grow your business," says Alfredo Ramirez, president and CEO of Austin-based Vyopta, a cloud video customer engagement company that secured a $500,000 revenue loan in 2013. Execs at his lender, Austin-based Next Step Capital Partners, don't have a seat on Vyopta's board, he explains, but the financiers observe board meetings and offer advice as needed, "like a VC, but without buying equity."

Financing through a Family Office

One option for financing that's often overlooked is the family office. Family offices operate as private companies that manage investments and trusts for a high-net-worth family or group of families. They're typically very private and misunderstood, but if you unlock the secrets to how family offices invest in new ventures and the criteria they look for, it could be the key to funding your business.

How a Family Office Could Help

Family offices are a particularly important source of capital for small-to-medium-sized businesses. According to the Family Office Club, there are currently more than 3,000 family offices in the U.S., and these offices often look at alternative investment opportunities—which could be your startup.

Family offices, which generally have a minimum of $100 million in assets, could be worth looking into as a source of funding for entrepreneurs.

While family offices can be elusive and highly selective, referrals, trusted networks, or entrepreneurship conferences may provide entry. The company seeking funding must also align with the family office's investment criteria and philosophy. Many have a predisposition to invest in companies directly or indirectly related to the core business on which their success is built.

Ultimately, any new investor is betting on both the business plan and the founder/CEO. Conversely, the founder/CEO needs to find and identify a new investment partner who has a long-term view and the time and interest to help propel the business forward.

If you're being introduced to a family office by a financial firm, there can be fees associated with the transaction. All investors will want to understand the exit strategy of the investment and clearly articulate that it is important.

If a family office chooses to invest in your business, you may find that family offices:

> Provide incredible connections
> Are able to take advantage of a situation where markets may cease to function in a regular manner
> Are more patient than institutional investors or private equity
> Appreciate how much work has to go into starting a successful company
> Serve as mentors

When Morten Middelfart went searching for seed investors for Social Quant, his Twitter analytics company in Tampa, Florida, his banker suggested pitching Atlantic Merchant Capital Advisors, a local family office. One informal meeting with the private investment firm, which manages the wealth of individuals and their families, was all it took to land Middelfart's venture a high-figure investment early in 2015, along with ongoing advice, customer introductions, and part-time office space.

Such experiences are rare, but they do happen, and more family wealth-management groups are betting on private equity deals. There are some drawbacks: Family offices can take longer to seal the deal than traditional angels and VCs, and they generally have a lower tolerance for startup failures, warns David McCombie III, founder and CEO of McCombie Group, a Miami-based private investment firm that has invested about $10 million in half a dozen startups in the past three years. But, he adds, many enjoy advising and supporting founders beyond simply writing a check. Plus, they have buckets of cash.

How to Find a Family Office

So how do you go about finding a family investment office to back your business? Not all family offices are so named, making them tough to pinpoint via a web or LinkedIn search. Some don't even have a website. To broaden your search, McCombie recommends creating a wish list of wealthy people you'd love as backers and using LinkedIn to identify mutual contacts to introduce you.

Networking offline is equally important. "Get out into the community first. Get to know everybody," says Mike Kawula, who joined Social Quant as CEO in April 2015. He credits that tactic with securing Social Quant's funding. It's best to let the investment community know who you are and what your company does before you go actively trolling for funding.

Once you've got some leads on family offices, call to ask whether they invest in early-stage companies, what startups their current portfolio includes, and what industries interest them. "The reality is, if you had a list of 100 family offices and personal contacts at each of them, only five or so would be legitimately interested in directly investing," McCombie says.

Diego Villarreal, who raised $60,000 in seed capital from a family office for his nightlife app, Banter!, warns that chasing after cold leads is a waste of time. "People say fundraising is a full-time job. But if you only go for the hot leads that might actually convert into investments, it's not," he says.

Cut to the chase by emailing an abbreviated version of your pitch deck to hot leads. It should be designed to grab their attention. "Three to four slides is plenty," says Jeremy Office, founder of Maclendon Wealth Management, a multifamily wealth-management practice in Delray Beach, Florida, that caters to entrepreneurs. "The idea is to avoid overwhelming them and instead intrigue them enough so they want a follow-up meeting."

If you get the meeting, let investors know you're attracted to their experience or interest in your industry, McCombie advises. "Emphasize that you're not just looking at them as another rich person, but you came to them specifically because you think they can add some value."

In other words, show respect for the fact that these families constantly get tapped for capital, and they'll be more likely to welcome you into their world.

Checking Out Philanthropic Venture Capital

At one point, nongovernmental organizations (NGOs) and charity groups were the only options for alleviating societal ills, but in today's increasingly interconnected world, we're facing more complex issues that require more innovative and sustainable solutions. This has led to the rapid upsurge of social entrepreneurship; now socially conscious entrepreneurs tackle local and global social challenges while generating profits.

Social entrepreneurship combines social impact and sustainable business growth, taking on social issues by using business principles to its advantage. In theory, social entrepreneurship is an amazing concept, but the practical process in progressing from an idea to a sustainable operation has critical challenges, in particular during the startup financing stage.

How Social Entrepreneurs Get Initial Financing

Typically, a regular startup would turn to the following funding sources: network investments, banking, equity debt, convertible debt, crowdfunding, and so on, with a relatively straightforward process for funding channels that are revenue model options. However, social ventures don't have the same flexibility as regular startup ventures when it comes to leveraging capital.

First, equity or VC financing usually expects an exit strategy that does not automatically exist in social ventures, which usually plan on staying in it for the long haul. Second, investors need to have confidence in your business concept. However, social ventures make assessing risk more difficult, given the unique nature of cultural and business resource issues and investor networks. Third, and most important, investors usually depend on comparable investment activity that helps validate an investment thesis around market opportunity and valuation levels. That doesn't exist in many social venture markets, where activity is a lot patchier and those markets have yet to demonstrate clear trends in delivering investor returns. All this limits the availability of capital in social ventures.

The Global Trend for Social Ventures Clearing the Financing Hurdle

To access capital, social ventures have to do several things, including conducting intensive market research to prove their need for funding and their ability to manage and expand their business. But funding roadblocks might still arise. If that happens, social ventures should look into the following three options: leveraging partnerships, philanthropic organizations, and social cause competitions and funds.

Revenue-sharing partnerships involve social entrepreneurs identifying a partner who can bring economic value to both parties. The partner may have intellectual value or property to contribute that adds value to the venture in a unique way. The beauty of this strategy is that it is a win-win situation for both parties.

Philanthropic money is a large pool of capital social entrepreneurs can tap into. However, the definition of philanthropic money has shifted over the years. Originally it meant simple donations, which are commonly seen today as an unsustainable method of giving. Today's new wave of philanthropy is called impact investing, a form of investing in which a measurable social or environmental impact is part of the goal, along with a financial benefit. For entrepreneurs, this source of capital is advantageous because it requires lower than market rate interest or return targets, and for philanthropists, a principal attraction is that the returned capital can be recycled into other charitable activities. The concept of impact investing is still evolving, however, and it will take some time until it can accommodate the growing number of social enterprises.

Finally, as in other industries, startup competitions, accelerators, angel investors, and impact funds provide valuable exposure and mentorship, which can lead to capital for social ventures. Good avenues to explore would be business plan competitions, such as the Global Social Venture Competition and the Hult Prize, as well as business incubators and accelerators like Echoing Green, Unreasonable Institute, and Endeavor Global. Since most social ventures get their start thanks to committed and passionate donors, the challenge for the social entrepreneur is to identify a sustainable model.

Example: How Pi Slice Got Funded

Genny Ghanimeh is the founder and CEO of Pi Slice, a web-based social platform for microfinance. Here's how it works at her company, in her words:

"In practice, what model examples do we have of social venture startups that are securing financing? At Pi Slice, when we went for our first funding rounds, we learned from meeting diverse investors to rely on all funding channels. From the beginning, we had some pre-seed angel money that helped us to get started, and allowed us with MicroWorld (www.microworld.org) from the group Positive Planet (www.positiveplanet.ngo) to build a revenue-sharing partnership model—we're big fans of partnerships and creating shared value.

"We also participated in different entrepreneurship competitions, as much as time and timing allowed us to—the exercise of preparing for a competition, being mentored, and presenting the case to the jury is very beneficial to reassess the model, whether one gets funded or not. We still needed money, so we approached philanthropy capital while still pitching the project, focusing on financial and operational metrics. At the end of the day, social investors or philanthropists, like any investors, need to know that you can be sustainable and scalable, and that you won't require any other emergency rounds of financing.

"Finally, we also engaged with VCs and set future milestones to pitch them at a time when they would be interested to come in—this is a very useful exercise to set standards and milestone achievements in foreseeing the growth of the venture. Our experience has taught us to knock on all doors and try all funding models, because each model has its own added value and can prove to be crucial for a new trend to be successful."

Warby Parker: How Four Entrepreneurs with Social Vision Secured Venture Capital

Fashion-forward friends Neil Blumenthal, David Gilboa, Andrew Hunt, and Jeffrey Raider aren't your bargain-basement eyewear types. The four University of Pennsylvania Wharton School alumni always preferred designer frames and lenses that ran about $500 per pair—a fact they lamented.

"Most glasses are marked up between 10 and 20 times what they cost to manufacture, and that just didn't make any sense to us," Blumenthal says. So they set out to refocus the industry.

The four started New York–based company Warby Parker (named for literary iconoclast Jack Kerouac's characters Zagg Parker and Warby Pepper) in 2010 and set out to design, manufacture, and distribute high-quality eyeglasses that would compete with those of major designers, with a retail price of only $95.

The former director of the New York nonprofit VisionSpring, Blumenthal had spent five years giving away glasses to impoverished people. Those industry contacts not only helped him line up manufacturing and distribution resources, but that philanthropic focus also led the partners to adopt a one-for-one donation model: For every pair of eyeglasses sold, one pair would be donated to someone in need.

Warby Parker offers hundreds of upscale eyeglass and sunglass designs, and even one monocle design. The challenge has been keeping product in stock, according to Blumenthal. Editorial coverage in *Vogue*, *Vanity Fair*, and *GQ* has helped orders to skyrocket, Gilboa says, as has word-of-mouth. In fact, more than 50 percent of new orders come through referrals.

For a time, the team resisted raising funding beyond its initial efforts from a variety of high-powered angel investors, including Joel Horowitz, former CEO of Tommy Hilfiger; Ashton Kutcher; Lady Gaga manager Troy Carter; and Ari Emanuel, co-CEO of talent agency William Morris Endeavor. Ironically, the more Warby Parker turned down venture interest, the more it was pursued, Gilboa says.

Lee Fixel, a partner at New York VC firm Tiger Global Management, heard friends raving about Warby Parker. He reached out through his contacts and was impressed by Gilboa and Blumenthal. "They had developed great products and figured out new and cost-efficient ways to build and market them," Fixel says. "This is a large industry that has been starved for innovation."

In turn, the Warby Parker team was impressed with Tiger Global's experience with ecommerce companies. Tiger Global led Warby Parker's $12 million Series A funding round. Warby Parker went on to do several more rounds of funding, including another round with Tiger Global, and other rounds with T. Rowe Price and General Catalyst Partners.

The firm forms "deep partnerships" with suppliers and has reduced the typical turnaround time for a new frame order to 5–12 days. Warby Parker is also working to ensure that suppliers have dedicated production facilities to meet the growing order volume.

Meanwhile, the company's philanthropic commitments have remained strong. It became a certified B Corporation and purports to be one of the few carbon-neutral eyewear brands in the world. "It was important to the four of us," Blumenthal says, "that if we were going to dedicate our life savings and our time to building an organization, we wanted to have a positive impact."

Inside B Corporations

B Corp status—granted by B Lab, a Wayne, Pennsylvania, nonprofit—has become a badge of honor for more than 1,600 socially and environmentally conscious businesses since 2007. Some of the bigger names to nab the certification include Ben & Jerry's, Patagonia, Etsy, Warby Parker, and New Belgium Brewing. In some states companies can up the ante by becoming a benefit corporation, a legal entity that requires business owners to consider employees, the community, and the environment when making decisions, rather than being beholden solely to profits.

Numerous studies in recent years have shown that consumers prefer to buy from companies that blend social purpose with corporate mission. But when it comes to doing good in the world, it's not always easy to tell which companies are legit. A 2013 survey from Nashville, Tennessee, marketing agency Good.Must.Grow. shows that 63 percent of customers don't always trust corporate claims of social responsibility. This is where B Corp status comes in.

To get certified, a business must score at least 80 out of 200 possible points in a 150-question online survey. Companies are rated on everything from energy efficiency to employee programs to corporate transparency. They also must submit to a phone interview, provide supporting documentation, and amend their corporate bylaws to include their commitment to making a positive social and environmental impact.

Funding Strategies for B Corporations

When Donnel Baird needed seed capital to continue developing his B Corporation in 2013, he figured impact investors were the ticket. One year and 250 investor meetings later, BlocPower—Baird's online marketplace that connects investors with clean energy projects in underserved communities—hadn't raised a dime.

In 2014, Baird, whose company is based in New York, decided to try his luck in Silicon Valley. There, he landed a seed round from VC firms Kapor Capital and Andreessen Horowitz, plus more useful advice than he'd received in the previous 250 meetings. "In Silicon Valley, they said, 'Oh, are you two guys with a laptop? Great idea. Let's invest.' I think they're just more accustomed to that," Baird says.

There are more than 1,600 certified B Corps—as certified by nonprofit organization B Lab—from 42 countries and more than 120 industries. As more for-profit startups become B Corps, it's worth examining how this designation factors into fundraising. Whether you're an aspiring B Corp or are already certified, here are the strategies you should know.

Look Beyond Impact Investors

Some experts advise focusing your roadshow on investors who specifically target socially conscious businesses. Andrew Kassoy, cofounder of Wayne,

Pennsylvania–based B Lab, disagrees. "Most investors aren't that interested in whether you're a B Corp," he says. "They're interested mostly in: Is this a really talented entrepreneur, and is this a good idea?"

Yes, you want to align yourself with investors who support your vision and values, but that doesn't mean a company that's mission-driven "has to go out and find a bunch of investors with Birkenstocks," Kassoy says. "There are plenty of mission-driven businesses that are raising money from mainstream venture capitalists."

Lead with the Opportunity

Your inclination may be to open your pitch with how your business model will help reduce pollution or feed the hungry. Quash that impulse.

"One of the mistakes we made initially was that we led with impact, talking about job creation, green energy, and the financial savings for low-income families," Baird says. He quickly discovered that even impact investors place a premium on profitability. "They're not willing to take a discount on their financial returns."

Diving headfirst into the profit potential proved a better route. "Then the impact side of the business becomes cool for the investors. They're like, 'Wonderful, I'm not just investing in Uber for dogs,'" he says. "It's frosting on their investment cake."

Commendable morals won't score a financing deal. Without a killer product, you're sunk, says Mark Fischer, founder and CEO of the B Corp credit card processing company Inspire Commerce, which offers special rates for charities.

"Our goal is to always get the product to a state where it would be funded by a VC or private investor because it's awesome," says Fischer, who has raised $750,000 in seed funds for his Boulder, Colorado–based company from friends, family, and angels. "The 'better for the world' conversation is one we have after the value of the product offering stands on its own."

Include Metrics

Some mission-minded investors will ask how you plan to measure your venture's impact, says Steve Schueth, president and chief marketing officer of First Affirmative Financial Network, a socially responsible investment advisor based in Colorado Springs, Colorado. Include these metrics—be it anticipated mouths fed, children clothed, or textbooks donated—in your pitch, and update investors on the data at least once a year.

Tapping into Alumni VC Groups

When Stephanie Lawrence began raising her seed round in the summer of 2015, one of her first calls was to fellow Dartmouth alum Mike Collins. They weren't old pals from the dorm, though. Collins was the lead manager of Green D Fund, an investment group that makes six-figure bets on startups with ties to Dartmouth. "It's a fantastic resource for anyone raising money," says Lawrence, whose company, Traveling Spoon, connects world travelers with vetted local hosts willing to make them a homemade meal. "Plus, it can be a great signal to other investors to have some of that early support."

Dartmouth alums aren't some rare, lucky breed. Passionate alumni of schools around the country are launching similar ventures, seeking to give back to (and profit from) their community. There's the UCLA Venture Capital Fund, Stanford Angels & Entrepreneurs, IrishAngels for Notre Dame, Xfund for Harvard, and others. And unlike traditional angel investors, these alumni like to get involved. "They are incredibly willing to help and be connectors, and that's rare for an investor that's taking such a relatively small percentage of the total round," Lawrence says.

Although some funds are independent, Green D belongs to a network of them: Collins also launched funds for Yale and the University of New Hampshire, and has plans to expand to Princeton and Harvard. These schools, he figures, have a concentration of high-net-worth graduates with fervent attachments to their alma maters, which makes investor recruitment easy. Why don't schools just do this themselves? Simple, Collins says: "Venture capital groups reject 95 percent of the startups they see. Schools don't want to reject 95 percent of their alums."

CHAPTER 11

Preparing for an Exit

So you want to sell your company or turn the reins over to relatives or employees? Planning your exit should begin long before you leave the building. This chapter walks you through the necessary steps and several possible scenarios.

Introducing Five Smart Exit Strategies

If your startup is your dream, why would you want to think about an exit strategy? It's going to be so successful and so much fun that you don't need to think about what comes after, right? Wrong. There are two very real and practical reasons why you need to plan your exit:

1. Outside investors want to collect their return. Remember that equity investments are not like loans with interest. The investor sees no return until he cashes out or the company is sold. Even three years is a long time to wait for a paycheck.

2. Entrepreneurs love the art of the start. Assuming your startup takes off, you will probably find the fun is gone by the time you reach 50 employees or a few million in revenue. The job changes from creating a "work of art" to operating a "cookie cutter."

In three to five years, you may well be anxious to start a new entity, with new ideas and spin-offs that have built up in your mind and a certainty that you can avoid all those potholes you hit the first time around. If your startup was less than a success, you'll definitely want to erase it from your memory. With that in mind, here are five exit strategies to consider:

1. *Merger and acquisition (M&A).* This normally means merging with a similar company or being bought by a larger company. This is a win-win situation when bordering companies have complementary skills and can save resources by combining. For bigger companies, it's a more efficient and quicker way to grow their revenue than creating new products organically.

2. *Initial Public Offering (IPO).* This used to be the preferred mode and the quickest way to riches. But since the internet bubble burst in 2000, the IPO rate has declined every year since. IPOs are not really recommended for startups these days—shareholders are demanding, and liability concerns are high.

3. *Sell to a friendly individual.* This is not an M&A, since it's not combining two entities into one. Yet it's a great way to "cash out" so you can pay investors, pay yourself, take some time off, and get ready to have some fun all over again. The ideal buyer is someone who has more skills and interest on the operational side of the business and can scale it.

4. *Make it your cash cow.* If you are in a stable, secure marketplace with a business that has a steady revenue stream, pay off investors and find someone you trust to run it for you, while you use the remaining cash

to develop your next great idea. You retain ownership and enjoy the annuity. But cash cows seem to need constant feeding to stay healthy.

5. *Liquidate and close.* Even lifetime entrepreneurs can decide that enough is enough. One often-overlooked exit strategy is simply to shut down, close the business doors, and liquidate. There could be a natural catastrophe, like 9/11 or COVID-19, or the market you counted on could implode. Make rules up front so you don't end up going down with the ship.

To some, an exit strategy sounds negative. Actually, the best reason for an exit strategy is to plan how to optimize a good situation, rather than get out of a bad one. This allows you to run your startup and focus your efforts on making it more appealing and compelling to the short list of acquirers or buyers you target.

The type of business you choose should depend on your goals, and the way you grow it should be aligned with your exit strategy. Don't wait until you are in trouble to think about an exit; rather, think of it as a succession plan.

Preparing Your Exit

When Vanessa Troyer and Chris Farentinos launched MailBoxes4Less. com in 2000, they didn't give much thought to how they'd exit their online mailbox distribution company.

All that changed in 2006. Recognizing the huge growth potential in manufacturing high-end mailboxes for builders and retailers, the Los Angeles couple decided to channel all their efforts into a second business, Architectural Mailboxes. This meant selling the highly profitable MailBoxes4Less.com to free up the necessary funds.

It wasn't a scenario most entrepreneurs envision when they think about exit strategies.

"No one was sick," says Troyer. "We didn't want to retire. Investors weren't saying, 'I'm done.' There was no reason to sell the business."

But sell the couple did, garnering more than $1 million for the venture they'd founded years earlier with just $25,000.

It was the right move: Today, a couple decades later, Architectural Mailboxes continues to grow, with products available at Lowe's, Home Depot, Amazon, and Target, among other stores.

Hoping to follow in Troyer and Farentinos' footsteps? Experts say the best way to ensure you leave your company when and how you want—with money in hand—is to start plotting your exit strategy now, even if you're still developing the business plan. Sadly, study after study shows that a majority of entrepreneurs have no exit strategy whatsoever.

If that sounds familiar, don't fret. You're about to get a crash course in preparing for two of the most common ways to successfully exit a business: turning the reins over to a relative and selling the company.

Succession Planning vs. Selling to an Outside Party

Planning your exit strategy is about making "a proactive series of decisions" instead of merely reacting to unexpected events like a heart attack or an economic downturn, says Ted Thomas, former managing partner of Sun Exit Advisors, a business transition planning firm in Chicago.

"It's almost like the military: Before you go in, you want to know how you're going to get out," Thomas says.

The idea is to put in writing when you see yourself leaving your business, how much income you need to walk away with, and how you see yourself transitioning out. Do you envision yourself eventually downshifting to consultant? Growing the business to sell it? Grooming an heir to take your place?

If your hope is to keep the business in the family, experts say now is the time to have the tough conversations with your spouse and children about whom you want to succeed you—and whether they're even interested in the job.

"If you have buyers coming to look at your business, one of the first things they're going to ask is, 'Have you talked to your family about this?'" says Terry Mackin, managing director of mergers and acquisitions at Generational Equity, a Dallas-based firm that helps middle-market companies plan their exit strategy. "They don't want to come into a situation where the family is at odds about whether the business should be passed along."

"One of the greatest mistakes people make is assuming that a family member will want to or be able to take over the business," says Jack Garson, business attorney and author of *How to Build a Business and Sell It for Millions.* "Rather than trying to fit a square peg into a round hole," he says, sometimes the best way to provide for an heir is to "sell the business to somebody else and give the money to your kid."

How to Sell Your Business

If you do see selling as your exit, you need to focus your energy on creating a business that buyers will want. This means working on your profitability, competitive edge (so you stay profitable), sustainability (so you survive economic downturns), scalability (so the business grows), and corporate culture (so you hang on to good people), Garson advises.

"If you've got all this," he says, "people will be banging down the door to buy the company."

Finding the Right Advisors

As glamorous as selling your business may sound, entrepreneurs who've been there will tell you that it's an incredibly stressful, time-consuming process fraught with dozens of moving parts and truckloads of paperwork. If you don't hire the right financial, legal, tax, and business advisors to help shepherd the sale through, you're doing yourself a great disservice.

"The mistakes you could make just getting the tax part wrong could cost you 50 percent of the proceeds of the sale," Garson says.

Along with an accountant and an attorney well-versed in business sales and acquisitions, plus a personal wealth manager, you'll probably want an experienced professional in your corner who can broker the deal—namely, a business broker or an investment banker.

"If you're selling the business for $500,000, you're using a business broker. If you're selling the business for $50 million, you're using an investment banker," Garson says, adding that the cutoff point between the two falls in the $5 million to $10 million range.

Besides helping you set a realistic asking price and assembling the necessary marketing materials to entice sellers, brokers and investment bankers will discreetly contact potential buyers on your behalf.

"In general, sellers do not want anybody to know that they're selling the business," says business broker Sally Anne Hughes, a founding partner of Hughes Klaiber, a New York brokerage firm for midsize businesses. "If a client finds out the business is for sale, they might be concerned. Employees might also be concerned. Vendors might be concerned that they won't get paid."

To find a reputable broker or investment banker, get recommendations from your business advisors or entrepreneurs who've sold their business, Garson says. Be sure to vet any brokers or investment bankers you're contemplating working with, as they predominantly work on commission.

"Ask them the average size and price of the businesses they've sold," suggests Troyer. "If your company is worth $1 million and most of their sales are $7 million, you're not going to get much attention. You want to be with somebody who's selling businesses right around the price of yours."

Nipping Deal-Killers in the Bud

As with selling a home, the more time you spend getting organized and cleaning up eyesores, the more likely you'll be to sell your business without a hitch. (Likewise, should you keep the business in the family, the easier a time your successor will have picking up where you left off.)

"Think about potential deal-killers," Hughes says. "Before you put the business on the market, evaluate it with a broker, an accountant, or an attorney and try to fix any areas that may present problems."

For starters, Garson advises, your financial records and tax returns from the last three to five years must be crystal clear, and your contracts with customers, vendors, and employees must be current. Here are some other critical ducks to get in a row before courting buyers:

> ⟩ *Financials.* It's not enough to have your P&L statements and balance sheets shipshape, says Sun Exit Advisors' Thomas. "What's even more important is a cash-flow report—how much money you have in the bank, and what you anticipate coming in the next week to 60 days," he explains.

▷ *Expenses.* If you've been running personal expenses through the business, it's time to clean up your act, advises Generational Equity's Mackin. "We can talk about the legalities all day, but what happens is it depletes your business's value," he says.

▷ *Employee classification.* Incorrectly classifying employees as independent contractors isn't just a red flag for the IRS; it could scare off potential buyers, Hughes says. If you're unsure whether your people are employees or independent contractors, check with an employment attorney.

▷ *Operations.* If you haven't empowered any of your staff to run the show should you miss a month of work, now's the time, Thomas says. Nothing's more dangerous to a business than an operations manual that only exists in the owner's head.

▷ *Employee turnover.* The last thing you want is for key employees to leave while you're growing the company or negotiating a sale, Thomas says. Incentives like bonuses and stock options can help keep employees loyal.

▷ *Lease.* "Make sure you have a good relationship with your landlord, especially if it's a retail business or restaurant that's reliant on a particular location," says Hughes, who's seen deals implode when a landlord wouldn't let a buyer assume a lease.

▷ *Inventory.* If you have too much product, Hughes suggests liquidating it or writing it off and then cleaning up the warehouse before buyers visit.

▷ *Facility.* Clean, organize, and spruce up all your physical locations. "Your books can be spick-and-span, but if a person walks into your place and it gives them the creeps, it lowers their trust," Thomas says.

Negotiating Like a Pro

Another surefire way to kill a sale is to get greedy during the negotiations.

"One of the classic pitfalls is going for more money or more anything because you think you can," says Avi Karnani, cofounder of Thrive, a free personal finance website that launched in 2006 and sold to LendingTree in 2009.

To avoid this trap, Karnani suggests identifying the offer terms you need (say, $10 million), want (autonomy within the parent company), and that would be nice (a corner office).

"If you don't spend time in the beginning making it clear what your needs, wants, and nice-to-haves are, one of your stakeholders is going to say, 'I really think we can get $11 million,'" he says. "You don't want one person to become the holdout."

You also don't want to sell to the first prospect that comes along.

"You need to talk to a number of buyers," Garson says. "You want to create a lot of interest in the company."

When it comes to choosing a buyer, "it's not just about the money," Mackin says. "It's about the interaction and the trust factor you have with the buyer. Eight times out of ten, my clients sell for what is not the best offer."

Troyer can relate. She and Farentinos received five offers on MailBoxes4Less.com. They didn't go with the buyer who offered the largest sum; they went with the one who paid in cash and had the best business pedigree.

"You'd better believe in the person you're selling to because you'll be working with them during the transition," Troyer says. And depending on your contract terms, some of the sales proceeds could be tied to the business remaining successful.

Keeping Your Eyes on the Prize

Exiting your company may feel more like a marathon than a sprint. In a good economy, experts say selling a business takes an average of nine months. The due diligence alone—during which the seller combs through all your documentation ("it's almost like an IRS audit or a deposition," Troyer says)—can take at least six weeks.

While courting buyers, it's imperative that you stick to business as usual.

"It's crucial that your sales numbers stay up and that your expense numbers stay down," Troyer says.

It's also essential that your best employees focus on keeping the company running. Too often, Garson says, owners pull their rock stars from their posts and have them make the requisite presentations to potential buyers.

"It's a terrible thing to do," he says. Instead, he suggests, tap your investors or PR people to do these dog-and-pony shows.

"You have to continue to run the company as if nothing's going to change," Mackin says. "Buyers will want to see that you're running the business well. That's where you get the difference between selling the business and selling it at a premium price."

As for those discouraged by poor market conditions, "unless you have to sell, don't sell when the table's tilted against you," Garson says. "Work on building your business, making it stronger, and positioning yourself for the future. You only get to sell this business once, so you might as well do it right."

Succession Planning: Ensuring Your Business Continues to Thrive without You, by Brenton Hayden

Brenton Hayden founded Renters Warehouse in 2007, which went on to become one of the fastest-growing and highest-reviewed property management companies in America. This section offers firsthand stories and hard-won advice directly from Brenton:

Succession planning can seem daunting, maybe even depressing for some. After all, planning for someone else to take over after you're gone isn't exactly the most exciting prospect. It's easy to look at succession planning as the first step toward your imminent departure, and really—who wants to think about being replaced?

But if you're planning on retiring at some point, or even hoping to step back from having an active role in the day-to-day business in your company, then having someone ready and waiting to take over is tremendously important. It's crucial for your company's continued success.

I was 21 when I made the decision to retire early—perhaps a somewhat lofty ambition. After all, at that time, I had just founded my company, Renters Warehouse, and had less than a year of operating experience behind me. But it was a dream of mine, and so I set out to make it happen.

One of the first things I realized was that a company should not be dependent on any one person for its survival. So I got to work building and scaling my company, all while ensuring that it was set up to run independently of me.

My goal was to exit by the time I was 27. To do that, I needed a plan, $7 million after tax, and a successor to take over my role at the company.

In many ways, having an exit strategy in mind right from the start saved me from a significant amount of hassle. I was able to build my company brick by brick upon the idea of it being eventually run by someone else. My successor was able to easily fit into my shoes since the company wasn't ever designed to be totally reliant on me.

It took work, but the transition proved to be completely worth it. I'm proud to say that since my retirement, Renters Warehouse continues to grow and thrive.

Succession planning often takes years to facilitate, so it's important to start early. Here are a few things that helped prepare me for a successful exit.

Build a Solid Foundation

The key to a successful transition is to start building a solid foundation right from the start. Don't make the mistake of designing your company to depend on you—take this approach, and your company will be doomed from the moment you step out the door. Instead, try to work toward implementing clear systems that someone else will be able to seamlessly step into and follow. That way, when you exit, your company can function just fine in your absence.

Set Target Dates

Before you start looking at potential successors, it's important to commit to a target date. This is only fair, after all—it's hard to keep a potential candidate indefinitely without a timeline. Setting clear goals and milestones and working backwards from there allows you to break things up into manageable steps, and enables you to have a more effective (and actionable) plan.

Identify Key Roles

Identify crucial roles in the company that will need to be filled. It won't just be "your position." Depending on how you've scaled your company, you may need to think about the many different roles you have in the business. If you're sourcing your successor internally like I did, you'll need to fill their position as well.

Define the Competencies Required for These Roles

Decide what skills are required to fill the roles you've identified. Once you've established this, you can start assessing people based upon these criteria. I firmly believe that the best talent is often internal, but of course, this depends on the talent pool you have to draw from.

Plan for the Future

When sourcing talent or looking for a successor, it's a good idea to look to the future. Don't just think about where your company is now, but ask yourself where it's likely to be down the road. Which talent could help take your company further? Your ideal successor may be someone with an entirely different skill set to bring to the table.

Prepare Your Team

I believe it's important to have employees and management who are just as invested in your long-term vision as you are. Having a solid supporting team can help make the transition much easier for everyone. In order for your successor to thrive, your team has to be onboard, and fully support them.

Train and Empower Your Successor

While you may be lamenting the fact that you don't have a suitable candidate ready to step into your place, the fact is that there's no such thing as a "ready-now" successor. Even the best candidate will require some training to prepare them to take over your job. They'll get there in time.

The true litmus test is to give a potential successor some of your responsibilities. I sought to empower many of the key executives at my company. I gave them full access to the books and called on them for important management decisions. From the start I saw to it that they were involved with everything from branding to hiring decisions.

Implement Measurables

Finally, if you're planning on retaining some measure of involvement after stepping back, it's important to implement a system that will track how well your successor is managing the company. I use a scorecard system that uses major metrics to track the health of the company. These metrics include month-over-month growth, customer satisfaction ratings, average units under management per employee, new accounts, and canceled accounts.

Having numbers such as this holds people accountable, measures success, and gives you peace of mind when you review the numbers on a weekly or monthly basis. As a retired CEO, this allows me to stay out of the day-to-day operations of the company, but still gives me the chance to intervene if I see a problem.

Final Thoughts

Keep in mind that it's less about the plan itself and more about the result. Every succession plan will be different, and should be designed around the needs of your company. The best plans should flex and change along with your company's requirements.

Being able to sit back and watch your company continue to grow and thrive without you, while you get to relax and enjoy some of the rewards you've worked hard for, is a beautiful feeling. Far from holding you back, your succession plan can open the door for you. Just don't let it hit you on the way out.

All in the Family: Succession Planning

Family businesses are the backbone of economies around the world, constituting a crucial source of wealth and employment in both developed and developing countries. In the U.S., around 70 percent of all organizations and a third of companies listed in the S&P 500 are family businesses. They occupy an even more important position in the Middle East, where the PwC Global Family Business Survey has found that more than 80 percent of businesses are either run or controlled by families. This percentage is very high in Saudi Arabia, where 95 percent of all companies are family run, contributing approximately half of non-oil GDP and providing employment for 80 percent of total private sector employees (National Center for Family Business, Council of Saudi Chambers). However, many studies from around the world show that very few family businesses survive beyond the third generation, even in Saudi Arabia.

Due to their nature, family-owned businesses face many more challenges than their corporate counterparts. While succession is challenging for all businesses, it often becomes even more complicated when family relationships must also be considered. This overlap between business and family creates many obstacles to the management, growth, and sustainability of these companies. Blurred boundaries between ownership and management often lead to conflicts and jeopardize the companies' future.

While adopting sound governance practices can provide a valuable framework for family firms to address issues of sustainability and professionalism, they are usually not compulsory, as they are for large companies listed on the stock market. Family SMEs therefore rarely adopt corporate governance codes and principles, and even if they do, family emotions can influence strategic decision-making, and especially succession.

Rome Wasn't Built in a Day: The Succession Process

Succession is a lengthy process that should not be left to chance. Family businesses need to regard succession as an extended process of at least three years, with the roles and responsibilities of the predecessor and successor varying before, during, and after the succession.

Before the succession takes place, the predecessor must mentor their chosen successor, closely nurturing their knowledge about all aspects of the business. During the succession process, the predecessor should begin to delegate increasing levels of responsibility, particularly decision-making power, to their successor. Finally, the predecessor will retire, leaving the business completely in the hands of the successor. For this process to go smoothly, however, certain individual attributes of family members and interpersonal relationships within the family are important.

Attachment Issues: Predecessor Attributes

Reluctance to let go is one of the most significant factors in the failure of succession in family businesses. Leaders are often unwilling to plan for succession for multiple reasons, including an emotional attachment to the business, fear of retirement, loss of status, lack of power, or even a lack of diversions outside work. This attachment to the business leads many family business leaders to maintain a leadership (or "consultant") position, even after retirement. While their experience can be invaluable, this continued presence can be perceived as a lack of trust in their successor, adversely affecting the decision-making process and confidence of employees and leading to frustration from the successor, as they live in the old leader's shadow. This inability to transfer power can be described as an addiction, with all the negative consequences that this term suggests.

Taking Over: Successor Attributes

The willingness of a successor to take over is also crucially important in family business succession. Studies show the established leadership of family firms perceive commitment to the business as the most desired attribute in their future successor, ranking even higher than their competencies.

The human and social capital of the successor is also crucial. Formal education and experience outside and inside the family business are all widely recognized as being extremely important parts of succession development plans. However, in many cases, mentoring by the incumbent is the most effective way to build the successor's human and social capital. This provides successors with firsthand experience of all aspects of the company, allowing them to adapt to its organizational culture and build relationships with important stakeholders.

The Ties That Bind: Predecessor-Successor Relationship

The generation gap and personality differences are the most common reasons for disagreements to arise between the current leader and their chosen successor. To avoid this, family businesses must adopt a culture of trust and mutual respect, supported by open communication. This will allow for an effective transfer of knowledge and social capital and ensure the continuation of the business.

Lack of trust from the predecessor can profoundly affect the successor's development; lack of communication often results in a frustrated, uncreative, or even rebellious successor. Either will prevent a successful succession. Trusting the ability of one's chosen heir gives them confidence, which generally translates into greater productivity and achievement. Open communication helps prevent misunderstandings and results in clear intentions and expectations on both sides.

It Takes a Village: Family Relationships

Nepotism and sibling rivalry are common in failed succession plans, underlining the importance of a shared vision among family members, helping to keep the family united once the established leader steps down. Avoiding conflict between family members requires clear distribution of shares, roles, and authorities, as well as the decision to base compensation on experience and competency. Emphasizing family values, loyalty, and traditions can also play an important role in achieving a harmonious atmosphere and shared vision in family firms, all of which supports a smooth succession.

Handing over a business to the next generation is a real challenge to family businesses. However, it can be achieved by families working on their internal relationships to foster trust, open communication, and mutual understanding between family members. Poor senior management succession planning is one of the reasons many family businesses disappear before they reach their third generation. At the end, having strong, solid family ties can help facilitate a smooth intergenerational transfer of wealth and reduce conflicts within families.

Turning the Business Over to Next of Kin

Here's how to gauge whether the next generation wants to run your business and is up to the task. Handing down a family business is a dream of many entrepreneurs who want to see the business they started thrive in the hands of the next generation. But statistics show that succession can be riddled with challenges.

Only about 30 percent of businesses make it to the next generation. Wendy Sage-Hayward, a senior consultant at the Vancouver-based Family Business Consulting Group, says although many families may want to pass down their business, the succession process is often not thought through carefully enough to make the succession successful. Here are some handy guidelines to increase your chances of success:

> ▷ *Avoid holding the reins too tightly.* Founders have a tendency to hang on to control, not allowing their kids to have enough say or enough investment in the business. "The entrepreneur typically does have a fairly strong control-oriented personality," says Sage-Hayward. Entrepreneurial characteristics tend to be very independent, autocratic, and particular. It can be difficult for entrepreneurs to let go of those tendencies, but Sage-Hayward says that's exactly what needs to happen in order to have a successful succession.

> ▷ *Eliminate entitlement.* Just because your last name is "Jones" doesn't mean you should automatically get a seat at the Jones Company's boardroom table, says Sage-Hayward. She recommends entrepreneurs set expectations around how kids will get to participate in the family business. Often, kids will be encouraged to go outside the company for work experience and education so they can bring those experiences back into the family business.

> ▷ *Build the skill sets of the next generation.* One of the biggest mistakes Sage-Hayward says she's seen in family businesses is that the founders have been so busy working in and building the business that they haven't spent the time to work on building the skill set or engagement of the successive generation. "Working on the business means you're developing the next generation, engaging them, helping them get the kind of skills and capabilities that they need to take it over," says Sage-Hayward. Building stewardship in family members means holding regular family meetings to involve other family members in the key conversations so they understand the ins and outs of the business and are prepared to take it over when the time comes.

> ▷ *Consider whether the next generation wants to be part of the business.* Sometimes founders have a dream that their children will take over

the family business, but the children simply aren't interested. Sage-Hayward says this often happens when the founder shuts out the family from the day-to-day interactions of the business or is so busy building the business and not spending time with their families that the kids begin to resent the business and want nothing to do with it when they get older. Involving kids in the business at an early age in a positive way is the best way to ensure they will be enticed to join the business later on. Having discussions about what children's aspirations are and how the family business can help them achieve their goals is also important. "Succession planning isn't an event; it's a process," says Sage-Hayward. "And that process starts from a very early age, building work ethic, building the understanding of the business, and building the mindset."

≫ *Be prepared to let go.* Ruling from the grave is one of the worst mistakes entrepreneurs can make when handing a business down to the next generation. Trying to set up structures that will control what the next generation can do rather than allowing them to run the company will only cause leadership ambiguity and create a stressful work environment for those family members who are left to run the company. Founders should be emotionally and mentally prepared to walk away from the business completely when the time comes around.

Transitioning to Employee Ownership

Kim Jordan and Jeff Lebesch wanted to run a more democratic business. Rather than shoulder all the tough decisions themselves, the founders of New Belgium Brewing Company sought their employees' input early on. This meant cultivating what Jordan calls a "high-involvement culture" of engaged, enthusiastic workers and transparency with staff about all sorts of matters, including company finances.

But employee enthusiasm goes only so far, so in 1996 the pair created a phantom deferred compensation plan, at no cost to the staff of their Fort Collins, Colorado–based craft brewing company. (A *phantom deferred compensation plan* is meant to help retain key executives by giving them additional benefits beyond their regular salary and traditional deferred compensation plans.) Later, when they started an employee stock ownership plan (ESOP), they honored the original plan until all account-holders' ESOP balances were larger than their phantom balances.

When Lebesch left New Belgium in 2009, Jordan and the company bought him out, bringing employee-owned shares to 41 percent. After mulling succession plans, Jordan opted for full employee ownership. By early 2013, more than 500 New Belgium employees—Jordan refers to them as "coworkers"—assumed 100 percent ownership of the company. (Shares are awarded based on the recipient's percentage of the total wage pool.)

The benefits have been plentiful. "We have great retention," says Jordan, CEO. "Our turnover is under 5 percent."

The employee-owners are not only happy at work, she says, but are also a regular source of bright ideas. Business is hopping, too. New Belgium, maker of Fat Tire ale, is the third-largest craft brewer in the U.S. and the eighth-largest brewer overall.

New Belgium isn't the only business thriving under employee ownership. "If you look at the numbers, on average, ESOPs improve performance," says Loren Rodgers, executive director of the National Center for Employee Ownership (NCEO), a nonprofit organization with more than 3,000 members. Three decades of research show that ESOP companies enjoy higher sales growth, higher employee productivity, more job creation, and fewer layoffs, he adds.

But there's no guarantee that by forming an ESOP—or a worker cooperative, another type of business owned and controlled by employees— you'll reap the aforementioned rewards. If you're interested in running a more egalitarian company, here are four steps you need to consider.

Plan with Employee Succession in Mind

It's never too soon to ponder who you want running your company 5, 10, or 20 years out. "You're not going to own your company forever," says Alex Moss, founder and president of Philadelphia-based Praxis Consulting Group, which helps employee-owned companies improve corporate leadership, culture, and strategy. "You're going to either sell it or you're going to die owning it."

Contemplating who will take the reins when the time comes—and ensuring that all founders are in agreement—can save future headaches and heartache. You don't want to be forced to sell your baby to an investor or a competitor because you haven't thought ahead, Moss says. Instead, employee ownership offers a way for the company you built to remain independent and your corporate mission to stay intact.

If employee succession appeals to you, it's important to start running a more democratic ship now. Yes, transitioning to an ESOP or a worker co-op takes time and legal help. But a move to either structure also affects who you hire, how you manage staff, and which investors you partner with. The sooner you adjust your recruitment, management, and fundraising tactics, the easier the leap will be.

Open the Books

Although corporate transparency isn't a requirement for ESOP success, it certainly helps. "Our most successful members started treating employees like owners before they actually made them owners," NCEO's Rodgers says.

Jordan concurs. "I think people lose the power of feeling like an owner if they don't know what goes on behind the scenes," she notes.

That's why all New Belgium employees can access the corporate intranet "and look at the financials to see where the money goes," Jordan says. It's also why New Belgium managers share sales and financial performance figures with employees at monthly staff meetings and give progress and spending reports on big corporate initiatives, such as opening the Asheville brewery.

But you can't expect all new hires to know their way around budgets and forecasts from day one. That's why the brewery—whose staff includes production workers, microbiologists, chemists, and salespeople—incorporates financial literacy training into its mandatory employee orientation and devotes a portion of each monthly staff meeting to educating the team on accounting ratios, cash flow, and other financial topics.

"It's a commitment," Jordan explains. "You have to say, 'We're going to make it matter. We're going to dive into a lot with people. We're going to teach them to really get the benefit out of it.'"

Hire with Future Partners in Mind

Embracing a more democratic culture involves rethinking the hiring process. "We're not interviewing to hire an employee," says Blake Jones, president of Namasté Solar, a solar installation company in Boulder, Colorado, that became an employee-owned cooperative in 2011. "We're interviewing to hire a potential business partner."

The co-op's lengthy screening process starts with one meeting to assess a candidate's job skills, followed by another to determine whether the candidate would be appropriate for ownership.

"We don't want someone to come to work for us just because we're a great place to work," Jones explains. "We want people to be excited specifically about our company model."

John Abrams, founder, president, and CEO of South Mountain Company, an employee-owned architecture, engineering, and building company on Martha's Vineyard in Massachusetts, agrees. "Obviously, when we're hiring, we're looking for people who have the appropriate skill set. But in a way, that's secondary to finding people that we can imagine sharing ownership with in the future."

In this context, the old interview chestnut "Where do you see yourself in five years?" is more relevant than ever.

Also imperative: involving as many employees as possible in the hiring process. Besides helping to sort out the square pegs, this gives workers another layer of responsibility. "Not only do they feel like they are insiders and decision-makers . . . but they also feel some responsibility for making sure the new hires work out," NCEO's Rodgers says.

Cultivate a Culture of Democracy

Rather than shield employees from the big decisions, the most successful employee-owned businesses encourage staff to help make them. This isn't good just for employee morale; it's good for the company overall.

"When the people making the decisions bear the consequences and responsibility for those decisions and share the rewards, better decisions happen," Abrams explains. After all, frontline workers often see operational problems and business opportunities—and have ideas for fixes or new initiatives—that might not occur to management.

Contributing ideas may not come naturally to all employees. "You can't just take an employee who doesn't know a lot about business and expect them to be a good co-owner," says Jones, whose company has 60 owners. "You've got to coach them."

To that end, Namasté Solar's employees go through a one-year orientation period before they can buy stock in the company. During that time, potential owners (called candidates) are paired with veterans and encouraged to learn about the business and get more involved. Guided by their mentors, newbies must complete a 12-item curriculum, from understanding the corporate bylaws to meeting with the director of finance for training in reading financial statements.

Jones says the time spent grooming future co-owners is well worth it. "When you do that, the investment pays off tremendously in the form of engaged, passionate, empowered co-owners who will think and act like an owner the way that you do," he explains. "The secret to our success is that we've got [60 times] the entrepreneurial spirit [and] creative, passionate motivation that a sole proprietor would have."

* * *

Too often entrepreneurs are so focused on the value of the sale that they fail to adequately consider all financial implications, including whether the payout will truly cover their lifestyle and income needs. Two common financial oversights entrepreneurs make are underestimating how many of their everyday expenses are being subsidized by their business—medical and life insurance premiums, club memberships, vehicles, travel and entertainment costs, and so on—and overestimating the amount of after-tax investment income that can be generated from the proceeds of the sale.

Entrepreneurs also face the difficult challenge of giving up some control of their wealth—the wealth that, until the sale, was tied up in their business, an illiquid asset that they nonetheless managed. Moving that asset into a well-diversified investment portfolio, one that maximizes after-tax income while continuing to build wealth, requires ceding some control to experts, including, but not limited to, a financial advisor, a CPA, and an estate-planning attorney.

Transitioning through life's milestones isn't always easy. When you exit a business, the steps taken after securing the payout are as consequential as the ones taken to obtain it. In other words, don't rush it.

Funding Resources

They say you can never be rich enough or young enough. While these could be argued, you definitely can never have enough resources. Therefore, we present for your consideration a wealth of sources for you to check into, check out, and harness for your own personal information blitz. These sources are tidbits, ideas to get you started on your research. They are by no means the only sources out there, and they should not be taken as the ultimate answer. Research has been done on each company, but businesses do tend to move, change, fold, and expand. Please do your homework carefully, and then get out there and start investigating.

Government Resources

Business U.S.A.—For general information, (844) USA-GOV1 http://
business.usa.gov
Internal Revenue Service—(800) 829-4933, www.irs.gov
Minority Business Development Agency (MBDA)—www.mbda.gov
Small Business Administration—(800) 827-5722, www.sba.gov
U.S. Department of Labor—(866) 487-2365, www.dol.gov
U.S. Equal Employment Opportunity Commission—(800) 669-4000,
www.eeoc.gov

Accounting and Taxes

American Accounting Association—(941) 921-7747, www.aaahq.org
American Institute of Certified Public Accountants—https://www.aicpa-
cima.com/home
Association of Credit and Collection Professionals—(800) 269–1607, www.
acainternational.org
PrimeGlobal—International association of independent accounting firms,
www.primeglobal.net

Credit Services

Dun & Bradstreet—Provides business credit-reporting services, (800) 526-
9018, www.dnb.com
Equifax Credit Information Services Inc.—Provides credit-reporting
services, (800) 685-5000, www.equifax.com
Experian—Provides credit-reporting services, (888) 243 6951, www.
experian.com
Telecheck—Provides check-guarantee services, www.telecheck.com
TransUnion—Provides credit-reporting services, www.transunion.com

General Business and Finance Websites

Angel Capital Association—www.angelcapitalassociation.org
Bankrate—www.bankrate.com
Bloomberg Business—www.bloomberg.com

CNN Business—http://money.cnn.com
Entrepreneur—www.entrepreneur.com
Fiserv—www.fiserv.com
Investopedia—https://www.investopedia.com
Kiplinger—https://www.kiplinger.com
MarketWatch—www.marketwatch.com
The Wall Street Journal—www.WSJ.com
Yahoo Finance—https://finance.yahoo.com/

Accounting Software

AccountEdge Pro—www.accountedge.com
FreshBooks—www.freshbooks.com
NetSuite—www.netsuite.com
QuickBooks Pro—http://quickbooks.intuit.com
Sage One—www.sageone.com
Xero—www.xero.com
Zoho Books—www.zoho.com

Find Your Credit Rating

Annual Credit Report—"The only source for your free credit reports."
    Authorized by federal law, www.annualcreditreport.com.
Equifax—www.equifax.com/
Experian—www.experian.com/small-business/services.jsp
Free Credit Report—www.freecreditreport.com

Credit Rating Bureaus

Equifax—P.O. Box 740241 Atlanta, GA 30374, (800) 685-1111,
    www.equifax.com
Experian—(888) 243-6951, www.experian.com
TransUnion LLC—P.O. Box 1000 Chester, PA 19022, (800) 888-4213, www.
    transunion.com

Crowdfunding

Crowdfunder—www.crowdfunder.com

Fundable—www.fundable.com

GoFundMe—www.gofundme.com

Indiegogo—www.indiegogo.com

Kickstarter—www.kickstarter.com

Patreon—www.patreon.com

Peerbackers—http://peerbackers.com

StartEngine/Seedinvest—www.seedinvest.com

Out-of-the-Box Funding Options

Borro—Online pawnbroker, www.borro.com

Lendio—Matching small businesses with lenders, www.lendio.com

PawnAmerica—www.pawnamerica.com

YouPawn—www.youpawn.com

Lending

Business Loans—www.businessloans.com

CAN Capital—414 W. 14th Street, New York, NY 10014,
      www.cancapital.com

FedEx Small Business Grant Contest—https://www.fedex.com/en-us/small-
      business/grant-contest.html

Idea Café Small Biz Grant Center—www.businessownersideacafe.com/
      small_business_grants

Lendio—www.lendio.com

National Funding—www.nationalfunding.com

OnDeck—www.ondeck.com

Small Business Administration—https://www.sba.gov/funding-
      programs/loans

Small Business Innovation Research—www.sbir.gov/about/about-sbir

Women's Center for Entrepreneurship Corporation—www.wcecnj.org

Books

Crack the Funding Code by Julie Robinette, Amacam, 2019

Crowdfunded by Mark Pecota, independently published, 2020

Founders at Work by Jessica Livingston, Apress, 2008

Six-Figure Crowdfunding by Derek Miller (Author), Noelle Pugh (Author), Dylan Todd, Joy Ho, Boom! Studios, 2018

The Lean Startup by Eric Ries, Crown Business, 2017

The Startup Owner's Manual by Steve Blank and Bob Dorf, Wiley, 2020

The Tax and Legal Playbook: Game-Changing Solutions for Your Small Business Questions by Mark. J. Kohler, Entrepreneur Press, 2015

Write Your Business Plan: A Step-By-Step Guide to Build Your Business by the Staff of Entrepreneur Media and Eric Butow, 2nd edition, Entrepreneur Press, 2023

Online Startup and Funding Courses

Build Your Business without Breaking the Bank
https://www.udemy.com/course/build-your-business-without-breaking-the-bank/

Create a Damn Good Business Plan
https://www.udemy.com/course/create-a-damn-good-business-plan/

Fund Your Business
https://www.sba.gov/business-guide/plan-your-business/fund-your-business

How to Write a Business Plan
https://www.sba.gov/business-guide/plan-your-business/write-your-business-plan

Kickstarter: Crowdfunding Tips and Tricks to Fund a Campaign
https://www.udemy.com/course/hackkickstarter/

New Venture Finance: Startup Funding for Entrepreneurs
https://www.coursera.org/learn/startup-funding

Glossary

Accelerator. A program or organization that provides resources for startup businesses typically including short-term resources like funding, networking, office space, training, and mentorship. Accelerators are similar to incubators, but tend to involve strict time limits and are usually shorter-term relationships.

Accrual accounting. An accounting system that recognizes revenue when earned and expenses when incurred; income and expenses are recorded at the end of an accounting period even though cash has not been received or paid.

233

Angel investor: A private investor who invests personal wealth into a young business in exchange for convertible debt or equity. They may offer additional help such as networking or expertise.

Benefit corporation. Also known as a B corporation or PBC (public benefit corporation), this is a legal for-profit entity that requires business owners to consider employees, the community, and the environment when making decisions rather than being beholden solely to profits.

Bootstrapping. Funding as much of your own business as possible.

Break-even. The point where expenses and income are equal.

Business plan. A written summary of how a business intends to organize an entrepreneurial endeavor and implement activities and procedures necessary and sufficient for the business to succeed.

Capacity. Capacity or cash flow represents your ability to generate income that will pay your debts.

Cash accounting. An accounting method that recognizes revenue and expenses when cash is actually received or disbursed rather than when earned or incurred.

Cash flow. An accounting term that refers to the amount of cash that is received and spent by a business. It is not a measure of profitability; a profitable company can fail because of problems with cash flow.

Chattel-mortgage contract. The equipment becomes the property of the purchaser on delivery, but the seller holds a mortgage claim against it until the amount specified in the contract is paid.

Collateral: Property or assets offered as security in a loan agreement. The collateral may be lost if the loan is not repaid.

Conditional sales contract. A contract in which the purchaser doesn't receive title to the equipment until it's fully paid for.

Contribution margin. The amount of revenue available to pay fixed costs and profits after paying direct costs and variable costs.

Corporate venture capital. A traditional venture capital firm raises money primarily from institutional investors and high-net-worth individuals, while corporate venture capital uses cash reserves from a parent company to fund new endeavors.

Crowdfunding. The process of raising money to fund what is typically a project or business venture through many donors using an online platform, such as Kickstarter, Indiegogo, or Crowdfunder. The fundraising window is usually finite, and the fees and rules vary across platforms.

Debt financing. A method of financing a business that relies on borrowing to fund the initial activities of the business.

Debt load. How much debt you carry vs. how much credit you have.

Equity: The value or interest held in a business. Assets minus liabilities.

ERISA. The Employee Retirement Income Security Act of 1974, which enables employees to be responsible for their own retirement plans.

Factoring. Another way to stretch your money. It involves selling your receivables to a buyer, such as a commercial finance company, to raise capital and is very common in industries, such as the clothing industry, where long receivables are part of the business cycle.

Fixed costs. An expense that remains constant regardless of a change in the level of a company's business or income.

Incorporation: The creation of a separate legal entity for purposes of business. Responsibility and liability shift from the people personally involved to this entity when a company incorporates.

Incubator: Similar to an accelerator, an incubator provides support and resources for startups. The main difference is that incubators may start much earlier, even at the idea stage, and may stay involved longer, up to months or years.

Intellectual property (IP): As with physical property, intellectual property refers to exclusive legal rights over ideas and other mental creations, such as inventions, designs, written works, and images. Copyright, patents, and trademarks are examples of types of intellectual property.

Intrapreneurships. Incubators or accelerators developing potentially profitable ideas and offering supportive environments for entrepreneurs, only within the confines of a big company.

Leasing. Paying for only that portion you use, rather than for the entire purchase price.

Merger and acquisition (M&A). This normally means merging with a similar company or being bought by a larger company.

Microfinancing. A small $10,000 to $50,000 loan, as defined by the Small Business Administration of America (SBA).

Overhead. Fixed costs plus variable costs.

Pitch slam. Competitions in which entrepreneurs try to wow the judges with the best pitches.

Revenue loan. A loan that is repaid with a percentage of a business's ongoing revenue instead of as a recurring periodic payment, as is the case with a typical loan.

Royalty loan: A loan made in exchange for a percentage of future royalties earned by a particular intellectual property.

Seed round / Seed funding: Early-stage funding, usually the first influx of outside funding to a startup besides personal funding or that of friends and family. Seed funding aims to help get the business off the ground in its infancy.

Series A funding: The first substantial round of investment into a startup after seed funding.

Seller financing loan. A loan in which the seller "lends" the buyer a percentage of the sale price.

VC / Venture capitalist: An investor, group of investors, or company that advances funding for a startup business in exchange for an equity stake in the business.

Warrant. The right—but not the obligation—to buy shares of stock in a company at a preset price before a certain amount of time elapses. Warrants are often used to attract investors.

Index

237

clean energy, 123
Coelho, Norah, 58–59
collateral, 46–47, 51, 53, 234
college alumni investment groups, 204
Collins, Mike, 204
competitions. *See* contests
conditional sales contract, 34, 234
Conser, Russ, 99
consumer health care, 185
Conte, Jack, 143
contests, 10, 77, 78, 85–93, 198
contract templates, 73, 74
contribution margin, 234
convertible notes, 64, 65, 66, 72
Coolest Cooler, 129
Cooper, Steven, 162
corporate venture capital, 191–192, 234–235
Cote, Gary, 161, 163
Craigslist, 28
credit
    equipment purchases, 34
    factoring, 33
    graduated payment mortgage, 33
    home equity loans, 33–34
    letter of credit, 33
    trade credit, 32
credit cards, 42, 43, 47
credit reports, 40, 50
credit scores
    business credit scores, 43–45, 47
    personal credit scores, 39, 40, 41, 50, 52
    SBSS scores, 43–44, 50
Cronin, Nick, 20
Crowdfunder, 128, 144
crowdfunding

all-or-nothing model, 128, 131, 144, 148
call to action, 137
described, 10, 127–129, 235
early momentum and, 138
emotional investment and, 130–131, 133
equity-based, 145–146
feedback and, 134
finding manufacturers, 134
funding goal, 131–132
inclusive language and, 146–147
incorporation and, 149
Kickstarter, 127, 128, 130, 131, 134, 138–140, 144
marketing budget and, 135–138
marketing companies for, 135
pain points and, 131, 133
PR firms and, 136–137
promotion and, 132
Regulation A+, 145–146
rewards and, 131, 132, 139
social media following, 149
statistical failure of, 128, 135
top ten platforms, 142–144
updates and, 132
videos and, 130, 149
women and, 146–147
Crowd Supply, 144
customers, as investors, 71–73
cybersecurity, 183–184

D

Dartmouth, 204
Davis, Stephen, 121
Davis, Will, 75, 76
debt financing, 235
debt load, 235